POPULAR CRAFTS

GUIDE TO
EMBROIDERY

This book is dedicated to Gloria Sharp, who has given a home to many of my pieces and appreciates all of them, good and bad. She has also accompanied me around more needlework shops than anyone should be asked to walk round.

POPULAR CRAFTS

GUIDE TO

EMBROIDERY

S U E   S H A R P

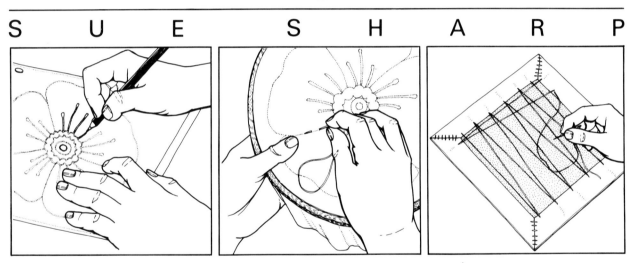

ARGUS BOOKS

Argus Books Limited
Wolsey House
Wolsey Road
Hemel Hempstead
Hertfordshire HP2 4SS

First published by Argus Books 1988

ISBN 0 85242 922 3

Phototypesetting by En to En, Tunbridge Wells, Kent
Printed and bound by Richard Clay Ltd, Chichester, Sussex

CONTENTS

Acknowledgements

The publisher and author would like to thank J and P Coats Ltd for their help in supplying projects for this book.

INTRODUCTION

INTRODUCTION

Like many other skills, embroidery has been in and out of fashion this century — picked up and put down according to the dictates of the day. But it is only in recent times that embroidery and its plainer cousin, sewing, have been at the whim of fashion. Until recently, in many countries it has been a necessity to make and finish clothes, household linen and decorative objects by hand without the aid of sophisticated machinery. In some other countries, this is still the case and learning to sew isn't a leisure activity but essential to the family's economy.

In many ways we are lucky that we can turn to sewing and embroidery as a hobby or interest that can be explored and enjoyed without the pressures of need pushing us on to finish this shirt so we can begin a child's skirt. People that embroider out of interest rather than necessity have the luxury of taking time to choose fabrics and colours, selecting patterns and stitches and working and experimenting at leisure; using their skills to relax rather than regarding them as part of a household chore.

The reason for embroidery going in and out of vogue are as many as embroidery stitches themselves. A reaction against 'home or hand made' and towards the products of increasing technology certainly contributed as did the reluctance of women to participate in something that could be seen as 'womens' work'. I had problems with this myself — as a woman who worked and was financially independent and proud of her ability to stand alone as an individual, my interest in sewing rested a little uneasily with this image. It seemed as if I was conforming to a role that I had already rejected — especially as I first became interested in embroidery at 19, an age when interests like needlecrafts are seen as something that your gran does.

I'm glad to say that I soon got to grips with this rather warped view and decided that part of individuality was being able to choose for oneself and if that choice included embroidery, so be it.

I don't mean to make light of the responsibilities of modern women and I can see why embroidery doesn't appeal to many people — but I think it is a shame that, at times, we are in danger of losing skills for the wrong reasons and without many people getting the chance to participate in something that can offer such fun and enjoyment.

The pleasures of creating are many and the pleasures of embroidery include many creative elements; colour, texture, shape and skilful execution. The satisfaction of completing a piece and seeing it framed or finished is also highly rewarding. But apart from anything else there is the satisfaction of working on a small pincushion or a mammoth wall hanging, using a few simple stitches or a full palette of effects, following a kit or designing yourself, working in an odd idle moment or devoting a weekend — and knowing that it's *yours*, something that you have worked and that has answered a need for you. And, I bet, economic necessities aside, this is what our ancestors got out of it too.

CHAPTER ONE

AN HISTORICAL PERSPECTIVE

A SHORT HISTORY

Sewing as a skill has been around since the first animal skins were joined together with thongs to make a warm covering for a chilly early man and the need for sewing for clothes and home is easily indentified amongst all societies in the world.

The need for decoration however, is another thing entirely — decorating with fancy stitching is time consuming and can be costly when specially prepared threads and fabrics are used, particularly when spare time and money are not readily available. But richly decorated clothes and linens demonstrate many things — wealth, religious or ceremonial significance, skill and particularly, an appreciation of the beautiful, an aesthetic awareness of the pleasure of a beautiful object.

Early societies that discovered how to make thread and fabric also discovered how to embroider — the Chinese had dye workshops as early as 3000 BC. The workshops produced thread for weaving and embroidery, coloured with natural dyes, leading to complex and sophisticated silk embroidery that glorified the rulers and gods.

Small pieces of ancient embroidery still exist, the oldest over two thousand years old. Most surviving pieces from this time are on clothes or have religious significance — some of the oldest secular work, worked as an historical document rather than for practicality or glorification, is the Bayeux Tapestry, worked in wool on linen and using just a few stitches. Although lacking in perspective or even anatomical knowledge to our more sophisticated eyes, it shows a clear and imaginative version of the series of events up to the Battle of Hastings. It was commissioned by the Bishop of Bayeux, illustrating the constant and close link between church and embroiderer.

Wherever embroidery is worked, it always shows something of the style of living of its time. Most societies use the materials that are closest to hand; silk in China, wool fibre and thread in Mediterranean countries with sheep whilst areas that grew cotton used it for their textiles. The designs worked and the items made also reflect important considerations — religious symbols are used on Eastern prayer mats whilst girls in India still sew age-old designs in gold thread on red cloth for their wedding saris.

Whilst all societies have traditional techniques and designs, these have been adapted by ideas from other parts of the world — increased travel swapped styles and enriched the native heritage. We usually regard embroidery as woman's skill, where embroidery is or was worked to earn money or for ceremonial purposes, but men also often participate.

Until the eighteen hundreds, embroiderers in most countries worked to traditional motifs or adapted existing designs to their work. With the advent of printing more ideas were available, usually of naturalistic design, which were copied. Transfer inks were developed in the nineteenth century producing a new range of designs for the embroiderer.

British embroidery is the result of a strong embroidery tradition and there is evidence to suggest that the art was used long before the Norman invasion of the country. One of the most distinctive styles is English work, which died out six hundred years ago (with some examples still surviving) using silks and metal threads. The Church and royalty were keen customers for the workshop output. The designs were mainly Biblical in nature although some work was copied from contemporary sources.

Samplers were popular in this country from very early times, worked in silk and metal threads in early days and using texts, natural and geometric forms. Wools and cotton threads were introduced later and crewel work, using wool, was very popular in Jacobean times. The range of stitches increased from the straight stitches of satin stitch to more complex forms like braid stitch, buttonhole stitch and french knots.

Although many women sewed from necessity, many girls were taught to sew because it was an acceptable way for a girl to pass her time productively — that is, if they were daughters of a better-off family. Less fortunate girls had to contribute more positively to the family finances!

Embroidery for pleasure had early fashions too; a form of wool work originating in Germany became a great craze in Britain and in America. Berlin work was worked with brightly coloured wools following a colour chart, which normally depicted stylised fruit, flowers and some geometrical motifs. It became popular because the charts were in colour — a new development from the ordinary graphs that just showed stitch placement. The advent of artificial dye also contributed, as a wider range of bright — not to say garish — colours were available. Amateur embroiderers in the 19th century also worked 'needlepainting' where the background was painted in water colour and the main focus of the design embroidered. Art needlework, which followed later, used designs by such eminent designers as William Morris.

There are several types of traditional embroidery in Britain that have been done for centuries and for which British embroidery is justly famous; smocking, whitework, broderie anglais and the lace-type embroidery that is worked in particular in Ireland and Scotland.

These traditional styles of embroidery have been added to over the centuries by techniques and ideas from all over the world. The European cross stitch is very popular with many embroiderers whilst the straight stitches of Florentine embroidery rely on their colour for vivid effect and whose origin is obvious. Techniques like these have been taken into the repertoire to form an almost international style that is modified and used with the traditions of the home country.

Despite the opinions of some pessimistic observers, embroidery remains a joy to many people — but perhaps the way they use it has changed. Whilst there are still many people who like to devote long hours to their embroidery projects, it's not possible for everyone to have the time or patience for really classic pieces of needlework. The advent of quicker, more fun pieces that use ready counted threads in fabric, a smaller scale or adapted techniques means that enthusiastic sewers with less time or money can still enjoy their hobby, whilst the growth in original design and experimental techniques can be used by those at the forefront of developing the frontiers of embroidery. Both aspects can co-exist to increase the numbers for whom embroidery is an important part of their life.

CHAPTER TWO

MATERIALS AND EQUIPMENT

You don't need a wide range of expensive tools and equipment for embroidery and needlecrafts, but once you get involved you are likely to start collecting useful sewing things. It's helpful to keep them together so that they don't get used by other members of the family — it's amazing how things can 'walk' into the toolboxes and school bags of non-sewing relatives!

As with most things, it's usually worth buying the best quality you can, but don't be put off by this — generally speaking the equipment is reasonably priced and it's items like scissors that are worth investing in to the best you can afford.

NEEDLES

There are three basic types of needle for hand embroidery. Always use the most suitable needle for the job; thread should pass easily through the eye of the needle without fraying as you work, blunt ends and large eyes are used for canvas work and a fine, sharp needle will be used for fabric that needs to be pierced, and for finer thread.

TAPESTRY

Tapestry needles are blunt and have a large eye for carrying thicker threads. The most common sizes are 14–18 but sizes 14–26 are available. This type of needle is used for canvas work and for counted thread embroidery when the threads of the fabric are not pierced and the sewing is done into the spaces between the threads.

CREWEL

These needles are sharp and long with a narrower eye. They come in sizes 1–10 but size 4 upwards are most commonly used. Crewel needles are the type most often used for embroidery, standard and freestyle stitchery.

CHENILLE

Chenille needles are also sharp but are thicker and longer than crewel needles. They have a large eye for carrying thick threads and are used for bold stitching and taking couching threads through fabric. Available in sizes 14–26 but 18–24 are mostly used.

Apart from these three basic types you will also come across and sometimes need;

Sharps   Have a small round eye and are fine for general sewing.

Betweens   Very fine small needles used for hand quilting — used by some people for general sewing.

Darning   Needles which are blunt with a large eye. They are used for working thick threads, ribbons and decorative strips like leather thongs.

Beading   These are very fine and long and are used for threading beads.

THREADS

It's important to consider the fabric you are using and the effect you want to create before buying threads. Think of colour, texture, thickness, matt or shiny, man-made or natural? Also consider the finished piece — will it need to be washed or dry cleaned? — most embroidery threads are dye fast and cotton is easily washed. Wool is probably better dry cleaned. Metallic and unusual threads might be unpredictable — to save spoiling a lovingly-worked piece work a sample and wash or clean it.

You can calculate thread requirements by working a sample and estimating coverage for a set length or skein of thread sample; it is worthwhile to buy all the thread you need in one go as different dye lots can vary despite the very best efforts of the manufacturer.

Virtually all threads are identified by a band or marking with manufacturer's details and colour number. Try not to lose these and if you transfer thread to any of the commercial or home made thread 'keepers' make sure you transfer the information. I can speak from bitter experience when I say that you won't remember the details and nothing is more frustrating than trailing around shop after shop and going through drawer after drawer trying vainly to match a small length of thread.

COTTONS

Stranded embroidery cotton   Comes in a large range of colours from several very reputable manufacturers. It consists of six loosely twisted strands which can be split to use the number of strands best for a particular project. It is used in many types of embroidery and is probably the most familiar embroidery thread.

Soft embroidery cotton   A lightly twisted five strand matte thread (in contrast to the glossier stranded thread) which is used complete. It is therefore thicker and is usually used on heavier fabrics. A very good colour choice.

Coton perlé   Or pearl cotton, is a twisted two-ply thread suitable for most embroidery as it comes in a range of three thicknesses. It has a sheen to it and is available in a good range of colours.

Coton à broder   A smooth embroidery floss with a shiny finish. The range of colours is not as wide as, say, stranded cotton but it is a useful medium weight thread which can add variety to work. It can be found in two different thicknesses, but white is available in several thicknesses for specialised work and techniques.

WOOLS

Tapestry wool   A tightly twisted four-ply wool which is used complete for canvas work and for some freehand sewing. Available in a wide range of colours.

Crewel wool   A finer two ply wool which is very strong and used for canvas work and freestyle embroidery. The strands can be separated for finer work. Subtle and wide colour range.

Persian wool   A three strand wool, loosely twisted. Each strand is two-ply and can be separated and used as one or two strands. It is used for canvas work and free style embroidery and comes in a wide range of colours.

SILK

Silk thread for special effects or for working a fine, intricate piece is available, but, as you might expect, can be expensive. You may need to hunt around specialist shops to locate it.

Silk floss   Or Filo floss, consists of six strands of silk which can be divided up for use.

Twisted silk   A twisted thread which has a high sheen.

Silk can also be used for tacking together fabrics which are delicate and will otherwise show tacking marks.

LINEN

Although widely popular in Scandinavia and some European countries, linen thread is less widely known in Britain and America. Available as a thin even thread or a thicker, sometimes knobbly thread, it is either matt or with a slight sheen and is only available outside Scandinavia in a limited range of colours.

Also available widely in Scandinavia and in specialist shops in this country is Danish Flower thread, a range of threads in muted colours that were designed for working flowers and plants. It is a fine thread that is ideal for cross stitch.

MISCELLANEOUS THREADS

Chief in this group is metallic thread which comes in a range of thicknesses and can be either real or synthetic.

They can be difficult to use successfully and should be used with care in ordinary embroidery — although they add texture and interest they can 'take over' if used too much. However they can be used exclusively in some types of work, especially church embroidery. They often require special techniques to be embroidered successfully.

Ordinary sewing and machine cottons and threads can also be used and can add great effect to projects that rely on texture for its impact. It is always well worth experimenting with threads that are not specifically sold for embroidery but be careful with mixing types — it may make laundering difficult.

Other options include knitting wool and rug wool although uneven or knobbly threads are not really recommended unless you are trying to get a special effect — they can be difficult to work if not uniform throughout. Special effects can also be obtained with raffia, leather thonging and string — again their use needs to be carefully considered and experimented with to ensure the right results.

FABRIC AND MATERIAL

Most of the fabrics used for embroidery fall into three basic types; woven, non-woven and knitted. By far the largest and most common group is woven fabric.

Woven material Fabric that is woven has warp and weft threads that are laid over and under each other whilst the selvedge is formed by the weft thread turning back.

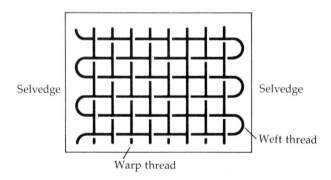

Selvedge

Selvedge

Weft thread

Warp thread

Even weave and plain weave fabrics are woven in the same way with weft and warp threads.

Woven fabric itself falls into three main groups for the embroiderer. **Plain weave** fabrics include most of the tightly woven materials with a smooth surface — examples are silk, calico, linen, hessian and organdie. This type of fabric is used for surface sewing like crewel embroidery and freestyle embroidery using cottons and medium weight threads. Medium weight fabric is best, whether natural or synthetic (or a combination of both) and purpose-made embroidery cloth is available in a range of colours, although white and neutral colours like beige are most widely available.

Even weave These fabrics look very similar to plain weave types but have a major, crucial difference; the number of threads per square centimetre or inch is the same for both warp and weft threads (the threads that run up

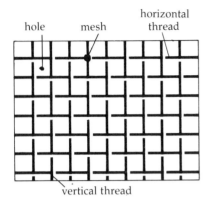

Plain single canvas, showing the holes and meshes that are counted and used for canvas embroidery.

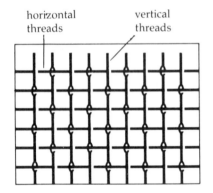

Interlock canvas uses two thin vertical threads that are twisted together and locked around the thicker horizontal thread.

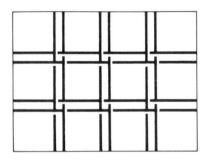

Double canvas uses pairs of threads that are woven together to form a strong stable canvas. Stitches can be made over double threads or single threads to vary the detail.

and down a woven fabric). This makes them ideal for techniques where threads are counted like cross stitch and blackwork.

Single even weave   Has single strands of crossing threads, whilst **multiple weave** fabrics have groups of threads intersecting (groups of two and four are most common). Block woven fabrics like these are woven with different numbers of blocks to the centimetre or inch; Aida fabric for example can have 8, 11, 14 or 22 4-thread blocks to the inch (2.5 cm) and is used widely for counted cross stitch, whilst Hardanger, with a much finer weave and used for Hardanger embroidery, has pairs of intersecting threads with 22 blocks to the inch. Even weave fabrics are also available in a range of colours and the increasing popularity of cross stitch has lead to a wide range of colours in block woven fabric.

Surface pattern   These fabrics have an evenly spaced pattern that can be used for guidelines in different types of embroidery. The pattern may be printed, like dots, or woven in like gingham or ticking. Woven fabrics of plain or even weave are best and can be used effectively for smocking, cross stitch and surface embroidery.

CANVAS

Canvas for embroidery is formed from open weave horizontal and vertical threads that produce evenly spaced holes. Most canvases are made of cotton or linen but some synthetic fibres may be used.

The gauge of a canvas is counted by the number of meshes, or points where the threads intersect, in an inch or 2.5 cm. To select the correct canvas, bear in mind the thickness of the embroidery threads you wish to use, the project itself and the design to be worked. The canvas should be completely covered when embroidered with no canvas visible.

There are different types of canvas available with *plain single* canvas the most common. The plain mesh is formed by a single horizontal and vertical thread crossing; how the threads intersect can vary. A plain canvas has the thread simply crossing as in weaving; in *interlock* canvas, each vertical thread is, in fact, two thinner threads which are twisted and locked around the horizontal threads where they intersect. This locked construction gives a firmer and more stable canvas, suitable for most stitches. Plain canvas does not work well with half cross stitch.

Double canvas is formed by the intersection of pairs of threads, both horizontal and vertical. This makes a very strong canvas and means that stitches can be adjusted to work over double threads or over single threads, forming smaller, finer stitches for detailed areas. The gauge of double canvas gives the count for both the number of double meshes per inch or 2.5 cm and the number of meshes if the threads are separated e.g. 10/20.

NON-WOVEN MATERIALS

These fabrics have the great advantage of not fraying when cut and do not have any grain, so they can be used and cut in any direction. Because of this, they often do not need hems and are usually very strong. The most familiar non-woven fabric is *felt*, which is available in a wide range of colours and by the metre as well as the school-day pre-cut squares.

Leather, vinyl and *suede* are also non-woven fabrics that can be used for embroidery. These are, however, less easy to handle and work than felt, although some are now washable. This type of material is usually used for garments and is probably best handled by experienced embroiderers who are more proficient at working and less likely to spoil very expensive materials.

KNITTED FABRICS

Knitted fabrics are looped together and usually look like the right side of stocking-stitch wool knitting. Because of this, the fabric stretches easily and therefore this type of fabric is not very suitable for many types of embroidery — it is almost impossible to successfully work surface or counted stitchery. It can be used for smocking and quilting, but it is suggested that you work a sample first to test results.

Never be afraid to experiment with different fabrics and threads, as there are all sorts of combinations that work well in practice that might not seem to be right in theory. Whatever you decide on, make sure that you leave a border of at least two inches (5 cm) around the finished size to allow for finishing and framing.

Knitted fabrics have the threads looped together like the right side of knitted stocking stitch. This makes it unsuitable for most forms of embroidery.

PINS

Always use steel pins that are intended for dressmaker's use. I prefer the finest, longest pins I can get, usually sold as lace or wedding dress pins as they are least likely to mark material. If using very fine fabric that marks easily, you can use fine sewing needles like betweens as pins.

SCISSORS

Good scissors are one of the few essential tools to the embroiderer. Two pairs are best; a small sharp pair with fine points for cutting threads and trimming the back of work and a pair of dressmaking scissors with long blades. Keep your scissors sharp and don't use them for cutting paper or household tasks — they will blunt easily.

Which scissors you choose is up to you; many like the plastic handled type as they are comfortable and usually good quality — look for a good brand like Wilkinson Sword or Pikaby. Needlework or embroidery scissors are handy if threaded onto a string or strap through one loop — they can be hung around the neck and always to hand.

Pinking shears can be handy for cutting fabric too. Keep a separate pair of scissors for cutting paper for designs and patterns, don't use the dressmaking scissors you keep for cutting out fabric.

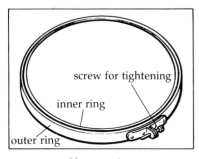

Hoop or ring

THIMBLE

Not everyone feels comfortable wearing a thimble, but they can increase your speed and comfort if you plan on doing a lot of embroidery, especially work mounted on a frame (see later this chapter and the next).

You can also try a fingerguard, a plastic sheath that covers the vunerable part of your finger. This can feel less clumsy as it doesn't completely cover the finger tip. If you are doing hand quilting, you will find some sort of protection almost essential.

Make sure that your thimble is of the right size — again, you might find leather more comfortable than metal and there are also some china and enamel thimbles that feel less bulky on your fingertip.

HOOPS AND FRAMES

Most embroidery can be worked held in the hand, but better, more even results will be obtained with the work held taut in a frame or hoop. Although it may seem clumsy at first, the results are usually so much better that a frame or hoop can be said to be essential.

Hoops consist of two wooden rings, an inner and outer. The outer ring can be tightened by a screw. Other versions can be made of plastic and Pikaby offer a type where the inner ring springs into place inside the outer, grooved hoop. Although simple hoops are held in the hand, there are table clamps and floor standing versions that release both hands for working. Hoops come in several sizes from a few inches (5 cm) to 12 ins (30.5 cm).

Slate and roller frames are used for working larger areas and work with two bars or rollers held apart by flat battens. The work is attached to the webbing that is stapled or pinned to the rollers; the fabric is laced to the battens at the side. Frames are measured by the length of the webbing on the roller, the smallest size usually being 18 ins (46 cm). For long pieces of work, the work is wound round the rollers to expose fresh fabric to be worked. Slate frames can be rested on the knees or table edge, but floor standing varieties are available as are trestles for resting the sides of the frame on.

You can also use a frame like a picture frame for attaching work to; either by staples or drawing pins. The fabric can also be folded over the edges and laced up with strong thread on the back.

Other items you might find useful include;

Stiletto   A sharp pointed tool for piercing holes. It is used for passing through very thick threads or for making holes for embroidering like broderie anglais.

Marking pens and pencils   For marking a design onto fabric (this will be covered in greater detail in the next chapter). Types include coloured pencils, transfer pencils that enable you to make a hot iron transfer from a drawing, felt pen types that leave a blue line that can be washed out with cold clean water and dressmaker's carbon paper and tracing wheel.

Rotating frame

Slate frame

Hot iron transfers   Available from commercial sources that imprint an embroidery design onto fabric.

Drawing materials   Ruler, set square and drawing board for designing. Masking tape is also useful for binding fabric edges.

A magnifier   Useful to see fine work clearly. One that hangs from a cord around the neck and leaves the hands free is best.

A tape measure   A flexible measuring tool.

A needle threader   For threading threads through needle eyes.

Blocking board   and T pins for finishing work (see the chapter on 'finishing').

   Household items like iron and ironing board will also be needed from time to time.

CHAPTER THREE

GENERAL METHODS AND TECHNIQUES

It's impossible to give hard and fast rules for embroidery, as everyone finds their own ideal way of working. However, there are some basic principles that will help ensure good results and some simple working practices that will make working easier.

PREPARING FABRIC

Before you start actually sewing there are preparations that, although they seem tedious and take up valuable 'sewing' time, make the difference between moderate and great results.

To prevent fraying of raw edges as you sew, bind using one of these methods.
(a) Masking tape.
(b) Hand oversewing.
(c) Turned edges that are machine stitched.
(d) Machine zigzag over raw edge.

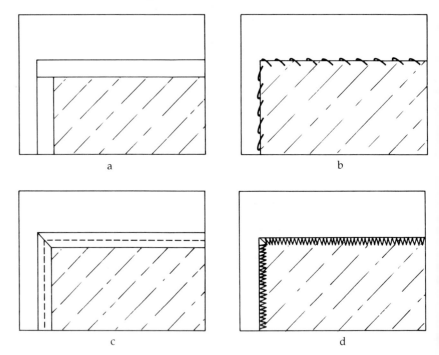

Iron the fabric that you plan to use. There should be a large margin (of at least 2 in (5 cm) around the actual embroidery size to allow for finishing. This doesn't allow for any fabric that may be seen inside the frame and surrounding the embroidered section, so plan carefully. Bind the edges of fabric that are likely to fray. This can be done by oversewing by hand or 'zigzagging' on a machine, binding with masking tape or using a commercial preparation like 'Fraycheck' which acts like a supple glue and stops threads working loose.

Mark the centre of the fabric by using running stitches sewn into the fabric or by marking with a pencil or pen. Some suggest folding and creasing along the centre — where the folds cross is the centre point. This does work but will not last while you work. If you are likely to need to refer to centre lines whilst you work, choose a more permanent method.

If you are using a hoop or ring frame, protect the fabric from slipping and damage by binding the inner ring. Use bias strip and overlap it slightly, but

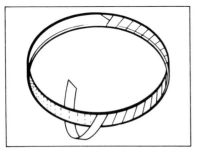

If you are using a hoop, bind the inner ring to prevent the fabric slipping and marking.

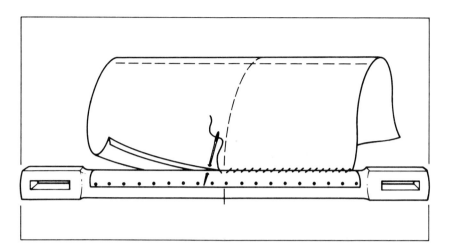

Match the centre of the fabric to the centre of the tape and oversew together.

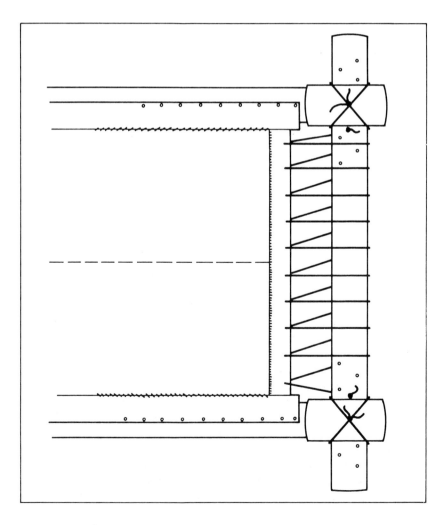

To secure the fabric to the side of the frame, bind the raw edge with tape or webbing and lace to the batten.

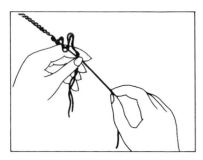

For separating wools gently, divide the first few inches and then pull on the strand you want, straightening the other strands as you go.

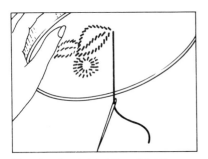

To untangle a twisted thread, let the needle fall freely to untwist and unwind.

To secure thread end when starting or finishing work.
(a) Work several stitches over the end of a new thread.
(b) Slide the needle and thread underneath the back of worked stitches when changing thread.
(c) Finish off by passing the needle and thread under several worked stitches on the wrong side.

make sure that the outer ring will still fit. A hoop will not always fit the complete sewing area, so you may need to move it around. If this is the case, you should protect already worked areas from the pressure of the ring with tissue paper or soft, clean fabric.

To place the fabric in the hoop, place the inner ring flat and lay the fabric over with the centre point in the middle. Place the outer ring over the fabric and push it over the inner ring. Make sure the material is taut and tighten with the screw. Material in a hoop will gradually loosen as you work and will need to be tightened.

To use a slate frame, fold a small turning (about an inch or 2.5 cm) to the wrong side at the top and bottom of the fabric. Position the centre of the fabric to the centre of the webbing and pin together from the centre out. Oversew through the top of the webbing and folded edge with strong thread. Use canvas tape about an inch wide (2.5 cm) along the raw edges at the side, tacking it on.

Rolling surplus fabric around the rollers, insert the battens at the side into the rollers. Then lace the fabric at the side through the tape to the battens using strong thread. Keep the fabric very taut to get best results.

THREAD

If you need to separate stranded threads (like stranded cotton or Persian wool), divide the first few inches into the number of strands you need. Pull apart — it's easiest, although not too elegant, to hold one group of strands in your mouth and pull gently with your hand on the other strands. Use your other hand to hold the undivided length.

This method works well with cotton, but you may need to be gentler with some wools. After dividing the top few inches, pull on the strands you want, straightening the surplus strands as you go to prevent tangling.

You can combine left-over strands together for further sewing, but make sure that they aren't twisted — it's a good idea to hold all thread from the top and let it untwist — thread that twists as you sew will be very difficult to work with. If you find, as you work, that the thread in the needle is beginning to tangle, let the thread fall with the needle at the end. It should spin round, removing the twist that has started to knot the thread.

Your thread will also be more inclined to knot and fray if you use too long a length in the needle — as it is drawn through the fabric it will begin

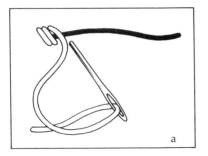

a

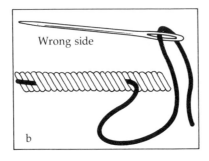

Wrong side

b

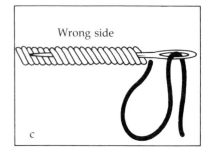

Wrong side

c

to wear. To avoid this, use lengths of thread a maximum of 20 in (50 cm) long.

To start a new length of thread or finish an old one, don't use knots or a bulky oversewing. This could show through on the finished piece and give a lumpy appearance. To start a new piece of embroidery, push the needle in about 2 in (5 cm) away from the area you wish to start sewing leaving a tail of thread hanging out. Bring the needle up where you want to start and begin sewing, catching in the tail as you stitch. Trim the end of the thread when it is secure.

To finish or start a new length of thread when sewing is begun, pass the needle under the back of several stitches on the wrong side, trimming off the end neatly.

If you want to carry on using the same colour thread in a slightly different area, it's alright to run the thread along the back of the work for a very short distance — too long a loop may pull tight or show through when sewn over. It's best to finish and start again if the new area is more than a few stitches away.

SEWING ACTION

One of the biggest complaints in embroidery from beginners is learning to stitch with two hands with a stabbing motion. If you use a hand-held hoop it's not easy to have both hands free, but with any anchored frame or hoop, you should endeavour to stitch in two movements, pushing the needle down with your left hand and passing it back up with your right. If you are left handed you may find it easier to reverse these instructions. Generally speaking stitches aren't formed by going into and out of the fabric in one movement as the fabric can be pulled and the stitches uneven. Although it may not be immediately comfortable, it is worth persevering with this stabbing technique.

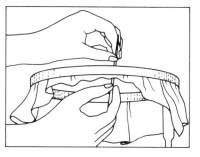

It's worth perfecting this stabbing technique of forming stitches as work will be more even and, when practised, quicker to work.

WORKING

With practice, you should be able to make the stitches with an even tension. Although the thread should be pulled through firmly, the fabric or canvas shouldn't pucker and, generally, you shouldn't be able to see the ground (fabric or canvas material that is sewn on) between the stitches.

When you start to sew, you need to position the design on the fabric. If you have marked the centre of the fabric and the centre of the design is marked, you can count the stitches out and up to show you where to start. If the fabric has the design marked on it there is no need to work out a starting position for yourself as you can follow the design. For details of transferring a design to your fabric, see later in this chapter.

If you are working on a frame and need to roll up a finished area to work a fresh area, you should protect the work already done by placing some soft clean fabric over it before rolling.

Your main efforts are, of course, to get a good result on the right side, but try to keep the wrong side neat too. Knots and oversewn areas and looped threads will all cause a bulky finished piece. Evenness is the real aim and

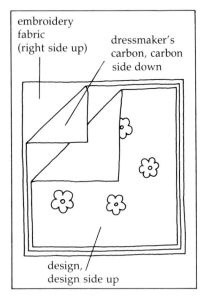

embroidery
fabric
(right side up)

dressmaker's
carbon, carbon
side down

design,
design side up

The 'sandwich' for transferring designs with dressmaker's carbon. All the layers should be well secured and the design centred on the fabric.

the best way to achieve this is with a working rhythm that is comfortable to work — and allows you to relax and enjoy your sewing.

TRANSFERRING DESIGNS

Many people are quite happy to work designs that are printed on their working fabric or to commercial charts, but many others find fun in designing their own work. The chapter on designing will help you if you would like to pursue this exciting route. It's likely that sooner or later you will want to put a design, either your own or a commercial one, onto fabric to embroider. There are several ways of doing this.

Remember that few counted stitch designs are put onto the ground fabric, they are counted from a chart where each square on the chart corresponds to a block or intersection mesh on the fabric. These are counted from the chart as they are sewn.

Evenweave fabrics and canvases usually need the design transferred. The most traditional method of doing this is called 'prick and pounce' which is very accurate although a little laborious. It is used on smooth fabrics but doesn't work well on canvas.

Lay the design onto a thick wad of fabric and pin down at the corners to stop it moving as you work. Using a special pricking tool, a fine point stiletto or a pin pushed into a cork, prick along the lines of the design, keeping holes close together and even. You can also use your sewing machine without thread and using a long stitch length.

Position the pricked design with the right side up on the embroidery fabric and pin securely down. Using a felt pad or roll, gently dab pounce powder (available from specialist needlework suppliers) over the design. Lift the pricked design off gently. Draw in the pounce lines with a pencil, fine paint brush and paint or marking pen, flicking away the pounce powder when done.

Tracing the design can be done if you can see through the fabric. Very fine fabric like organdie can be used in this way, as can canvas with its network of holes. The design to be transferred should have solid dark outlines. Tape it securely to a board or flat surface and tape the embroidery fabric squarely on top. Trace the design using a pencil, marking pen or dress maker's pencil following the lines of the design underneath. If you have access to a light box (a light source beneath a frosted glass panel) you may be able to use the tracing technique on slightly thicker fabrics — and a window on a bright day can come a good second to a light box but make sure that the design and fabric are well secured!

To use dress maker's carbon, sandwich the carbon paper, with carbon side down, between the fabric and the design, with the fabric at the bottom. Secure well, as a smudged design will result if anything moves. Draw around the design using a tracing wheel or a pointed object like a knitting needle. A knitting needle may give you greater control with curves and small details.

For designs without fine detail you can use running stitches to trace a design pinned on top of your fabric. Follow the design with small running stitches. Gently tear the design away leaving the stitches behind. This is a good method for highly textured sewing surfaces.

Most people are aware of commercial hot-iron transfers where the design is put onto the fabric from a paper that is inked with a design. Most transfers include instructions which should be followed. Make sure that the transfer doesn't move during ironing and check that the iron is at the correct temperature. If doubtful, try a test transfer with a small scrap of fabric first.

You can also make your own hot-iron transfers. Specialist shops sell pencils that, when used on a thin paper and ironed on, leave the design behind. Remember that the design will be reversed if you trace your design right side up.

AS YE SEW, SO SHALL YE RIP

It's inevitable that you will make mistakes. Some you can live with, some are too much of an eyesore.

If you have to remove stitching, it's important that you don't pull hard at stitches to remove them. You will pull the fabric and the replacement stitches won't lie right. Better to clip each stitch and carefully take it out than pull and leave fibres behind and an out-of-shape replacement stitch. Take out the stitches each side of the error so that you can work a small row of new ones, working at the same tension as the rest of the embroidery. Make sure that thread ends are well secured.

A stitch ripper with a small bobble on will pull out some stitching.

To avoid mistakes, work in a good light and use a magnifying glass for fine detail. A lamp that you can have over your shoulder like a spotlight will stop the rest of the family moaning about the bright light. It's counter-productive to try to work otherwise.

Other simple ways of avoiding mishaps are;

— check that your fabric is pre-shrunk. Most are, but imagine the horror of a precious piece puckering and curling after washing. Keep washing to a minimum — clean 'working practices' will help. Wash your hands before starting and keep away from grease.

— put work away when you have finished working on it for a while. Cover work in frames with a cloth — put small pieces in a bag — just a plastic one will do although there are some very pretty and ingenious work bags. Spilt coffee or dirty dog paws will ruin the piece and your interest in it!

— pull skeins of wool and thread from a cut end and pull gently, making sure that you keep the colour number band. If you are the sort of person that only has to look at threads for them to jumble into a knot, wind the skein around a commercial or homemade thread keeper. Commercial ones can be kept on a key ring type holder and have space for the shade number to be written. These can be worthwhile if you are using subtle colours with very close, matching tones as it can be very easy to use the wrong colour if the light isn't first class.

A WORD ON KITS

I've spoken to many people who are apologetic that they 'only work kits'. I wish they wouldn't think this is something to be ashamed of. Kits are convenient, nowadays very cleverly and beautifully designed and usually include everything you need. There's no rule that says embroidery can only be enjoyed the hard way — and no rule that says kits are any less well worked or enjoyed than a self designed piece that has taken years to produce. The point of a hobby or interest is that the individual takes what they need from it and this is no less valid if the work comes from a kit.

CHARTS AND PATTERNS

Unless you intend to design your own projects, you will also want to buy patterns to work to.

Many canvas and fabric pieces have a design already stamped on; canvases will often have the appropriate colours printed or painted on too. This makes working easy as you follow the guide on the canvas.

There is also a wide range of fabric items like tablecloths and linens with a design transferred or stamped on. These are usually for freestyle embroidery, although there are some stamped cross stitch designs too. These do not have colours marked, but are copied from an accompanying guide.

Hot-iron transfers are available, for transferring commercial designs onto your own fabric; these leave colour and thread choices up to you.

There is also a large selection of excellent books and publications with designs charted for you to follow. These cover the entire range of embroidery styles and techniques and often suggest colours and thread types.

You may also need graph paper for working out your own charts for counted stitches like cross stitch. This is used for plotting out patterns that you have designed yourself and are worked in the same way as the commercial charts that are available.

CHAPTER FOUR

DESIGNING

Many embroiderers are apprehensive about designing their own projects — usually considering that they can't draw well enough, or at all.

But drawing skill really isn't necessary; most embroidery designs depend on shape and interpretation rather than advanced drawing ability. Sources for designs are all around you; magazines, wallpaper, patterns of street railings, leaves, vegetables and household items. Often you won't want to make all of the object the design — look at an interesting part of it, narrow in on a section that offers texture and draws your attention.

Museums offer a rich design source as motifs, ideas and pattern can be taken from historical embroidered pieces. The Victoria and Albert Museum in London and The Costume Museum in Bath have wonderful exhibits that can spark ideas. But don't limit yourself to the costume sections — patterns can be found on pottery, household objects and coins for example.

DESIGN IDEAS FOR NON-ARTISTS

Ideas that are used in schools to stimulate creativity in children also work very well with adults — even for those who are convinced that they can't create.

Try the following ideas;

Cut patterns from geometric shapes. Cut out a circle, triangle, square, lay them over each other. Cut up, say, the circle into segments, spread out the segments, overlapping some, space others out.

Use drawing equipment like ruler and compass. Experiment with straight lines; evenly spaced, irregular, parallel and crossing to produce other shapes. Use a compass to draw different size circles, overlapping, perhaps used within each other. You can use cups, plates and jars if you don't have a compass.

Doodles can lead to all sorts of ideas. One of my favourite pieces is based on one of my recurring doodles — just a simple pattern of shapes locking together but it works. This just needs a pen and pad by the phone!

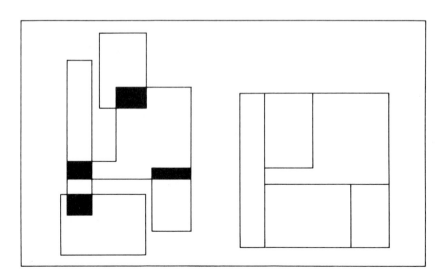

Cutting geometric shapes and rearranging them make unusual and striking modern designs.

Try dropping a length of string from a height onto a sheet of white paper. Look at the pattern it makes on the paper. Abstract or like a flower? Will a few extra lines turn it into something different again? Don't like it all? — pick up the string and try again.

Even ink blots can become a work of art. Use the childhood technique of an ink or paint blob on a piece of paper. Fold the paper in half and then open out.

DRAWING AND SKETCHING

If you would like to base your design on a sketch of your own, try to get into the habit of carrying a small drawing pad and pencil with you — inspiration can strike at unusual times. If you draw from life, remember that you aren't trying for a photographic image, you are capturing the feel and atmosphere. If you can't draw people, look at skylines and the patterns made by buildings. You probably won't want every detail, just the basic shapes and outlines.

Photographs and similar sources   You may want to work a design from a personal photograph or use a picture from a magazine — or even match

Lines drawn with a ruler and pen can be easily added to and other shapes placed on top to make a design that requires no drawing ability.

Two L shapes cut from card will help you to isolate a part of a complex design — this is especially useful for choosing designs from wallpaper, fabric or magazine pictures.

furnishings with a pattern from wallpaper or fabric. To help focus on an interesting piece, you might find it useful to cut two L shapes out of cardboard. Used as a frame you can move them about over the picture or pattern until you find a piece you like.

Again, you probably won't want all the detail that is on the original — you will be interpreting yourself and adding your own texture and colour to the project.

Once you have found your design, you need to transfer it into a clear outline, reproduce it to the right size and put it on the fabric you wish to use. Whatever method you have used to get your design, draw or trace it onto paper (tracing paper is probably best) using a black pen to give clear outlines. This is the basic design. Unless you are very lucky you will probably need to enlarge it or reduce it to the scale you wish to work in. This is easily done.

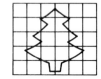

ALTERING SIZES

This technique is worth learning as it can be used for all sorts of things, not just your own designs.

It is done by drawing a grid over the picture to be enlarged. (If you don't want to draw on your original, draw the grid on a tracing paper overlay.) A grid of about 1 in or 2.5 cm is a good size. On another piece of paper, mark out a grid the size you want the design to be with the same number of divisions as the original. Copy the outlines in each square of the original onto the corresponding square of the other grid. This can be used to enlarge or reduce a design.

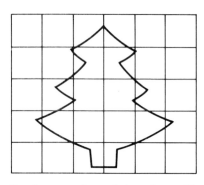

To enlarge or reduce a design using a grid, copy, box to box, the design lines from the original to the new grid.

This way of altering design size is also used for patterns in magazines and books. The instructions will usually give the grid size that the design should be transferred to.

Once your design is the right size, you may need to take a border all around to finish it off. To get a good 'turn' on the corner, you can use a simple trick with a mirror. Lay the border design flat, securing if necessary with tape or a heavy object. Using a small mirror like a hand-bag mirror with a flat edge, place it diagonally across the border at a point that will make a good turn. Hold the mirror upright to get a reflection of the border at right angles. You can try several areas of the design to get the best results. When happy, draw a line along the base of the mirror.

Trace the border up to the line drawn from the mirror. Fold the tracing paper along the mirror line and trace part of the border pattern onto the piece of folded paper. Open up the tracing paper to get the corner design.

Transfer the design to your fabric using one of the methods described in Chapter 3.

COLOUR, THREAD AND STITCHES

When choosing threads and stitches, the paramount consideration is the type of design you are working. A delicate floral pattern will demand finer embroidery threads and subtler colours than a bold geometric design

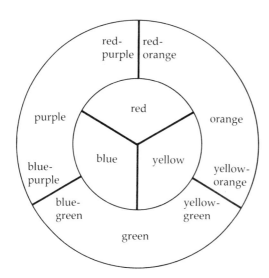

The three primary colours mix to produce secondary, contrasting colours. Bear these groups and their relation to each other in mind when you plan thread colours.

worked on canvas. Texture also plays a part — try matching stitches to get the types of textures in a landscape for instance.

Colours will make or break the piece you are working — however beautifully worked, discordant colours will always detract from the finished effect.

Self colour   Means that you will only use one colour, getting variety from thread thicknesses and textures. True self colour uses thread the same colour as the background fabric as in white work.

Monochrome   Tones of one colour on a different colour background. It's best to use light and dark tones on a medium colour background or medium and dark on a light ground. Tones that match too closely will detract from each other. You can use a contrasting colour amongst the monochromes for a very vivid effect, using it as a splash amongst the toning colours.

Polychrome   Means the use of many colours, and here you have to work hard to get the right balance between the different colours.

Consider how colours work to get the best results. **Primary** colours are red, blue and yellow. The **contrasting** colour to each primary is the mix of the other two primaries; red contrasts with green, blue with orange and yellow with purple. **Analogous** colours are colours that are similar; yellow and orange, blue and green.

Tones are light and dark hues of the same colour; shade is the degree or depth of a colour. The shades of two different colours like red and blue may be the same because they have the same depth of colour — but tones of a colour usually refer to just the one colour.

Bear these facts in mind when you come to plan the colours for your design — you are looking for a pleasing and harmonious effect. This doesn't mean limiting your colour range but using it wisely. You can always try colouring copies of your design with paints or pencils to experiment with different ideas before setting out to buy your threads — you may avoid an expensive mistake.

CHAPTER FIVE

FINISHING AND MAKING UP

When you have finished sewing your project, you should have an even clean piece of work that can be framed or made up into a cushion or whatever.

However, this isn't an ideal world and most pieces will be grubby, perhaps pulled out of shape if a frame or hoop isn't used and in need of a little work to get them looking perfect.

You can take your work to a specialist framer who, even if you don't want the piece framed, will 'block' the work for you. But it is possible to do it yourself and if only a little work is needed, there is no reason why you shouldn't get good results.

EMBROIDERY ON FABRIC

If the ground fabric and threads are colourfast and not going to shrink, you can wash the piece in cool water using a gentle detergent. One of the liquids sold for washing woollens is ideal. Wash the piece carefully — don't scrub or wring. Rinse thoroughly and place the work on a soft, clean towel to blot out the excess water. Don't tumble dry — leave to dry flat on a clean towel.

Use a clean, dry towel to blot the excess water from a piece of washed embroidery — do not wring it.

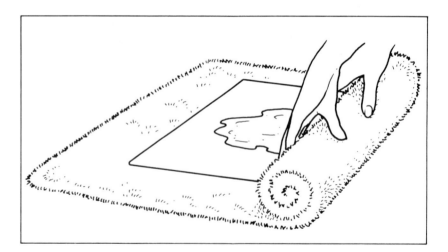

If you have any reason to think that the piece isn't washable, take it to a reputable dry cleaner or use a proprietary dry cleaning spray or stain remover.

If your work has kept its shape it can be pressed to remove the wrinkles and to straighten minor distortions. Pad the ironing board with a towel or several layers of soft fabric. Place the embroidered piece face down and press lightly, either using a damp cloth or pressing through a dry cloth if the piece is still damp from washing. Pull gently into shape if required.

Work that is badly distorted will need blocking. This technique is also used for work done on canvas that cannot be washed.

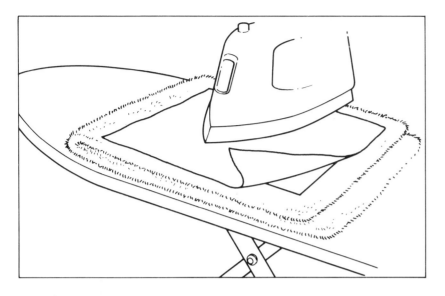

If the finished embroidered piece has kept its shape, or is only slightly distorted, press it gently through a clean cloth — gently pulling the project back into shape if necessary.

CANVAS WORK

Blocking is often more necessary on canvas work than on fabric embroidery as canvas is more likely to distort when worked.

For canvases that are only slightly distorted, lightly steam press the canvas on the wrong side. This will even out the stitched surface and correct the shape slightly if pulled gently. Let the canvas dry thoroughly.

It is not recommended that you wash canvases — the canvas itself can

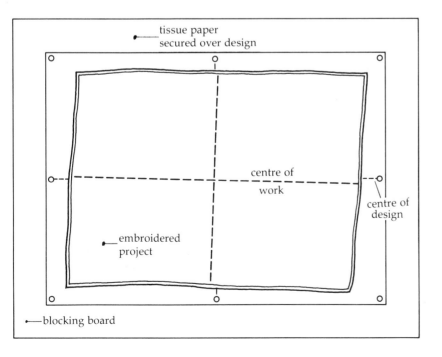

tissue paper secured over design

centre of work

centre of design

embroidered project

blocking board

If your work has become badly distorted, you will need to 'block' it. When the work is damp, it is pinned back into shape following the original design and ensuring that the centres of the worked piece coincide with the centre of the design.

pucker. If very dirty have it dry cleaned, otherwise sponge gently to remove surface dirt.

For work that is more distorted, you will need a board to 'block' on; a ⅝ in (1.5 cm) thick piece of soft wood or composition board is suitable. A piece about 2 ft (60 cm) square will fit most embroidered projects. Pad the board for embroidered pieces; it can be left for canvas work.

It helps to use the original pattern as a guide for blocking canvas work — place it on the board and cover with a piece of tissue paper. Pin or tape in place. Damp the canvas on the back — use a damp towel to wrap it in or sponge with warm water — and leave until the water has damped stitches and canvas. The canvas should not be dripping with water.

Pull the canvas into shape with your hands, stretching corners and edges. Place the canvas face up on the pattern, stretching the canvas, aligning the edges with the edges on the pattern. Pin with T pins or drawing pins, using a pin every inch (2.5 cm). Leave to dry thoroughly — if still out of shape, repeat the process until the canvas matches the pattern.

To block fabric embroidery, it helps to have a grid to pin the embroidery out to; mark out an inch (2.5 cm) grid with a ruler and indelible pen that won't run when wet. Soak the clean embroidery in cold water and lay on top of board, face up if there are raised and textured stitches, face down if the stitches are flat. Pin at each corner and pull out sides to get straight edges, using the grid as a guide. Leave to dry thoroughly before removing from board.

FRAMING AND MAKING UP

There is a wide range of ready made frames available in the shops at inexpensive prices. They are easy to use and will finish off a piece to be proud of.

To secure embroidery in the frame, it should be placed centrally on the thick card inner that comes with the frame (if there isn't one, cut one from card, a fraction smaller than the inner edge of the frame). Pin to the edge of the card to hold it in place — you can also secure small pieces with double sided adhesive tape. Turn the card and fabric over and lace the edges of the material together, working from the centre of each side towards the edges. Use a strong needle and thread. Cut surplus fabric away from the corners and hem neatly in place.

Place glass face down in frame if used (it will help protect the work from dirt and non-reflective glass will show off the work well), followed by a cardboard coloured matte if used. Put in the emroidery face down and close the frame with the outer backing. Secure with pins or tape.

Fabric embroidery can be framed cheaply and in a fun way with a wooden embroidery hoop. Select a size that shows all the work. Use it as it is or paint the outer ring with acrylic paints to suit a colour scheme. Lay the inner ring on a flat surface and place a square of clean co-ordinating or plain fabric centrally over it.

For a padded effect you can then position a circle of polyester or cotton wadding (cut slightly smaller than the ring diameter) on the fabric over the

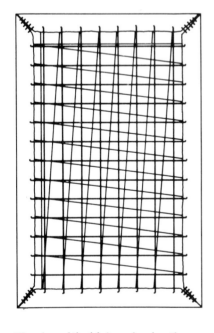

The edges of the fabric are laced on the wrong side of the mounting board and the corners sewn neatly in place.

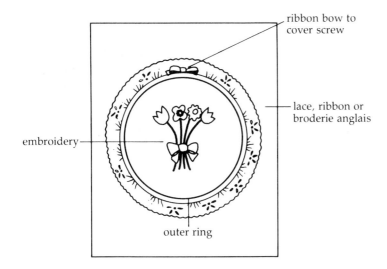

ribbon bow to
cover screw

lace, ribbon or
broderie anglais

embroidery

outer ring

*This is an inexpensive and fun way to
frame a piece of embroidery worked on
fabric. It uses a hoop or ring frame usually
used for working embroidery on.*

ring. Place the clean and pressed embroidery face up over the inner ring
and position the outer ring over all layers, making sure that the screw is at
the top. Push the outer ring down and tighten, keeping the embroidery and
backing fabric taut.

Turn over and place face down. Trim the fabric down to a $\frac{1}{4}$ in (6 mm)
and run a line of glue around the top of the inner ring. Stick the fabric to
the glue.

Tie a ribbon around the screw to disguise it — for extra effect you can
stick a fabric or lace ruffle around the diameter of the top ring from the
back.

CLOTHING AND ACCESSORIES

If you have worked your embroidery to set it into a garment, use it on a belt
or bag or make household items like cushions and tablecloths, it is best if
you work carefully to the size needed — otherwise embroidered edges
could fray and threads unravel if they are cut after completion. Mark out
the size with tacking stitches and work to this area.

If you do have to cut into an embroidered area, finish the cut edges with
machine zigzagging or several lines of straight stitch.

CANVAS EMBROIDERY

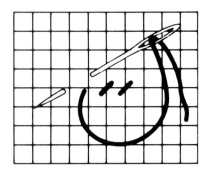

Tent stitch is the traditional 'tapestry' stitch and is used for pictures and furnishings. Because it is a small stitch, it is used where areas need delineating clearly as it can follow lines and shapes well.

Canvas embroidery uses the technique of covering an openweave canvas with stitches and is different from most other types of embroidery as the stitches cover the entire background, giving a fabric that is not only decorative but very hardwearing. For this reason, it is used for furnishings like rugs and chair seats.

The most common form of this type of embroidery is 'tapestry' where the design is worked in a plain, slanting stitch called tent stitch. This is often done on a pre-painted canvas, showing colour and stitch location. In fact, 'tapestry' is a misnomer — true tapestry is woven but early stitched patterns copied the designs of woven tapestries and the name has stuck.

CHOOSING CANVAS

Single mesh canvas is easier to work on and is available in a wider range of meshes than double canvas — usually from 10 threads to the inch (2.5 cm) to 24 threads to the inch (2.5 cm). 14 or 16 threads are the most common for chair seats etc. Use 18 threads to the inch (2.5 cm) for smaller objects whilst bold work may need 10 threads. Again, bear in mind what type of project you are working when choosing the correct canvas. Canvas work is not

Try a bold, geometric band inset into a tote bag — make the bag yourself using a commercial pattern or stitch the band onto a purchased one. Or work a square pocket and apply it after lining it. Using embroidery like this makes it a practical living craft.

always quick to work as all of the canvas is covered with stitches, but it doesn't pay to cheat by using a larger thread count and thicker thread than the work merits — delicate effects will be lost and the work will look out of proportion.

Double mesh canvas is also used for tent stitch but is also good for cross stitch and cross stitch variations. It's good for sampler type work too, as the double mesh means that you can vary the stitch size using the separated double threads. Double canvas can also be used for half cross stitch, which is difficult to work on single canvas.

The most popular sizes are 7/14 to 12/24 with 10/20 the most common.

Although you are probably most familiar with pictures or cushions in canvas work, don't ignore the many possibilities it has. Sections of canvas work can be inserted into bags and accessories like belts whilst household items like lamps, wastepaper bins and tissue box covers can transform a room's decor. Finished projects like spectacle cases, purses and diary covers will be hardwearing even if used a lot.

CHOOSING THREADS

The range of wools discussed in the chapter on materials are all suitable for canvas work and wool is the most usual canvas thread. However, embroidery cottons can also be used — stranded cotton is used on fine mesh canvas and soft embroidery cotton is suitable on larger thread count canvas. When choosing thread, remember that you are aiming to cover all the background canvas. Work a small sample if necessary of several lines square. You shouldn't see any canvas or holes on the worked sample and the stitches should be of even tension and not pulled tight or left loose.

You can also experiment using threads such as raffia, metallic thread and rug or knitting wool. If you use wools other than those designed for embroidery, use small lengths as there is a large degree of abrasion when the thread is pulled through the canvas as stitches are worked. Some threads will not be suitable if the finished object is subject to a lot of wear — metallic threads are an example.

Tapestry needles are best for canvas work as the eye is large enough to thread easily and the end is blunt, preventing the canvas being pierced. Size 18 is suitable for 10 and 12 gauge canvas, 14 for heavier canvases and 22 for fine work. The canvas shouldn't distort as you pass the needle through.

DESIGNS

If you like to work canvas pictures or natural designs, then you are probably familiar with pre-painted canvas, where the design and colours are painted or printed onto the canvas. These are usually worked in tent stitch or half cross stitch and are easy to follow.

If you want to design your own canvas work, bear in mind the kind of stitches you want to use. Tent stitch is a small, slanting thread that covers a single canvas mesh and can be used for delineating fine lines and areas —

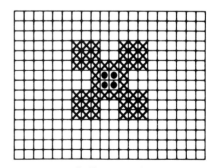

Using tent or half cross stitch, a chart or pattern will use a graph to place a stitch on every thread mesh — that is where threads cross. Each box on the graph is equal to one mesh.

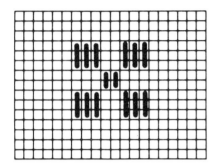

If ornamental stitches are used, the lines on the graph will equal the threads of the canvas with the intersections on the graph equivalent to the canvas intersections or meshes.

this is why it is used for natural forms and designs. Ornamental stitches are larger and give different textures (something that can only be achieved with colour and shading with tent stitch) but are not capable of following lines closely or complex shading — designs for ornamental stitches are less detailed and rely on texture and the basic lines of a design for effect.

To transfer your own design, you have more limited options than those available for embroidery. If the canvas is of a very open weave, you can trace the design from an outline in bold black lines by placing the design underneath and tracing the lines onto the canvas. You should use a waterproof pen for this. Once the design is on the canvas you can colour in areas using a paint brush and watered down acrylic paint to show colour placement.

You can also transfer the design to graph paper and colour in the boxes to show colour and stitch placement — the design is read from the chart as you sew. If you are using tent stitch, use each box as a thread of the canvas. If using ornamental stitches, each intersection on the graph is equal to a mesh on the canvas. You can colour in box charts in detail, line charts will need the area lines modified to fit the stitches you plan to use.

A QUICK WORD ON . . .
TENT STITCH AND HALF CROSS STITCH

These stitches are used for tapestry pictures and furnishings and are the most familiar stitch in canvas work. They are both worked diagonally and produce an even texture that can include colour shading and fine detail. Tent stitch is more hard wearing and less likely to pull the canvas out of shape as the piece is worked — but uses up more thread. If you are going to use this effect on single canvas, tent stitch should be used.

Half cross stitch uses up less thread but is difficult to work on single canvas — it distorts and the thread slips at the intersection points on the canvas. It can be made more durable by working over a laid or 'trammed' thread. If you have seen canvases for sale where lines of thread in appropriate colours are laid on the surface, this is tramming — a foundation thread that is covered by the embroidery as it is worked. You can also lay threads yourself for half cross stitch.

The eventual effect of both stitches is the same, but use the most suitable stitch for your work to get the best results.

For stitch diagrams see the directory for this chapter.

ORNAMENTAL STITCHES

These stitches are raised, textured and use a lot of wool to cover large areas — they are not suitable for fine detail. They are very good for interpreting texture and are often used for less traditional designs.

For ornamental stitch diagrams see the stitch directory for this chapter.

FLORENTINE EMBROIDERY

Strictly speaking this comes under the heading of 'ornamental stitches' but the characteristic shading and stitch effects are an area of embroidery on its own. Straight stitches singly or in groups are used to make zig zag patterns that are repeated to fill the design area. It is traditional that shades of the same colour or toning colours are used to give a rhythmical pattern.

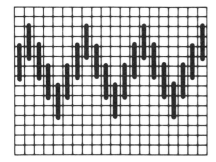
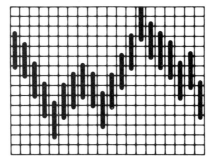

Florentine embroidery on canvas uses straight stitch worked up and down the canvas to form peaks and valleys. The stitch length and step can be varied to alter the peak height.

The Florentine pattern doesn't have to be regular — peaks of different size are made by varying the number of stitches between them and the amount of step.

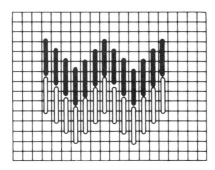

Once the foundation line of Florentine stitches is worked, the pattern is repeated above and below until the design area is full. Exciting combinations of colours can be used to create a harmonious pattern.

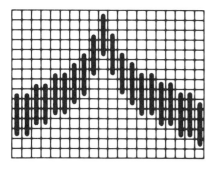
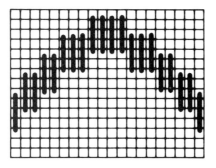

Stitches can be worked in pairs or curves to form patterns other than the basic zigzag.

Stitches are usually two to eight threads long and step up and down singly or in groups to form valleys and peaks of stitches. The step between the bases of adjacent stitches should be at least one less than the number of threads covered.

Florentine embroidery is about harmony and although it may seem repetitive, the number of variations and colour combinations are almost endless.

STITCH DIRECTORY

CANVAS EMBROIDERY

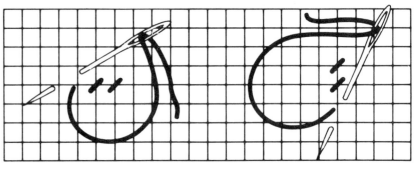

worked horizontally   worked vertically

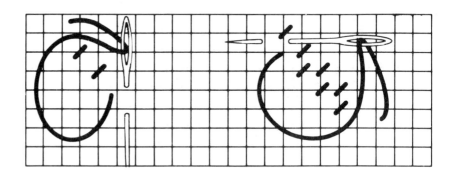

Basketweave — this is suitable for filling large areas of the same colour as it doesn't distort the canvas as you work.

Tent stitch

This stitch should only be worked on double canvas.

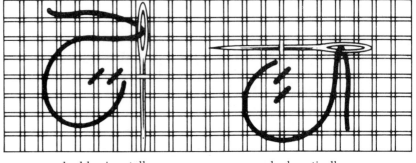

worked horizontally   worked vertically

Half cross stitch

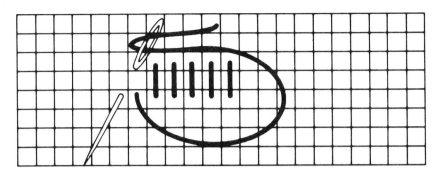

Straight or Gobelin stitch

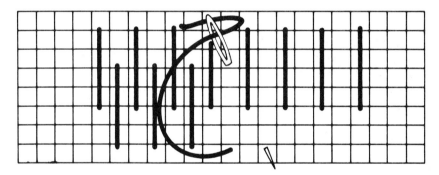

Gobelin filling stitch

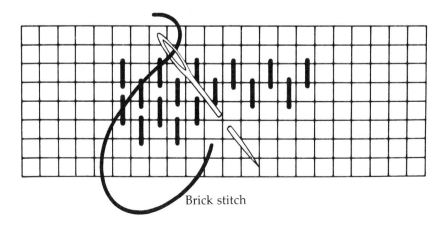

Brick stitch

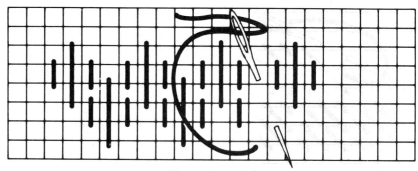

Hungarian stitch

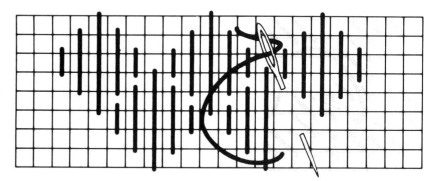

Hungarian Diamond stitch

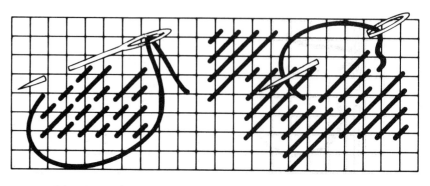

Mosaic stitch   Milanese stitch

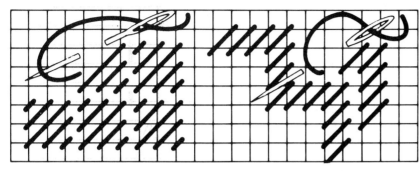

Scotch stitch   Byzantine stitch

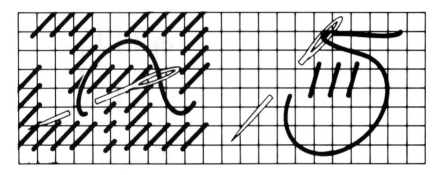

Jacquard stitch   Slanted Gobelin stitch

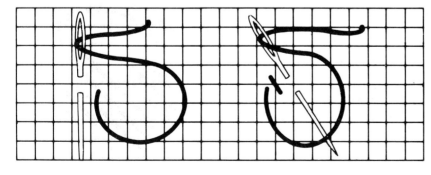

Cross stitch   — worked horizontally

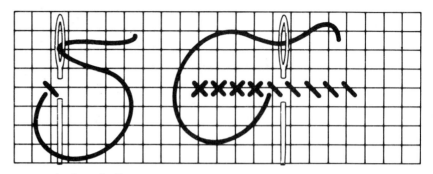

— worked vertically

— Worked in rows — a line of lower stitches worked and then crossed in a line.

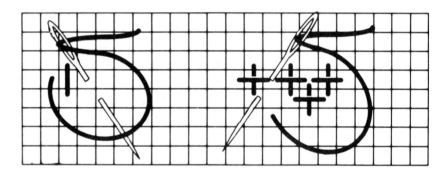

Upright cross stitch

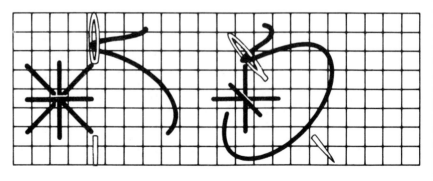

Leviathan stitch   Double straight cross stitch

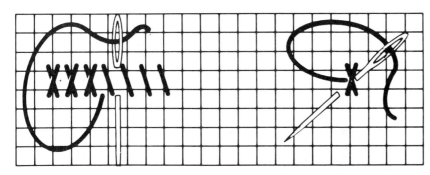

Oblong cross stitch   Oblong cross stitch with backstitch

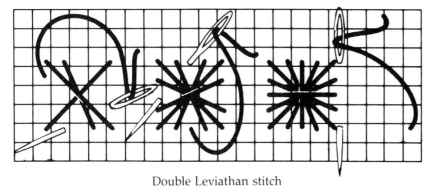

Double Leviathan stitch

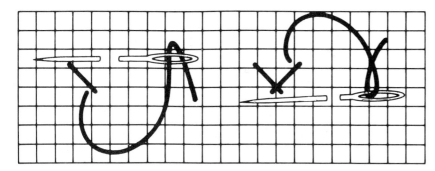

Herringbone stitch

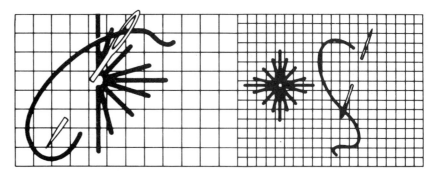

Diamond Eyelet stitch

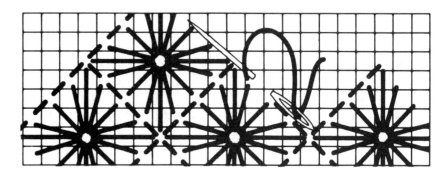

Diamond Eyelet stitch (with backstitch to close gaps around stitches).

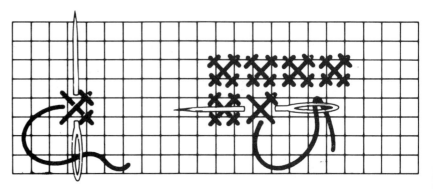

Rice stitch

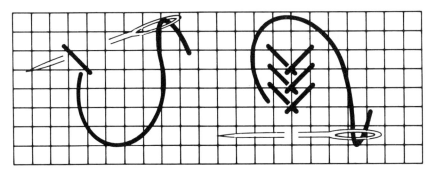

Fern stitch

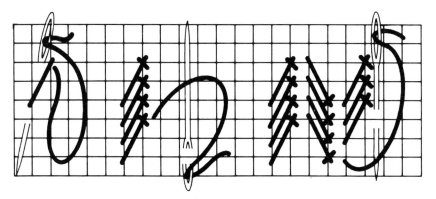

Fishbone stitch

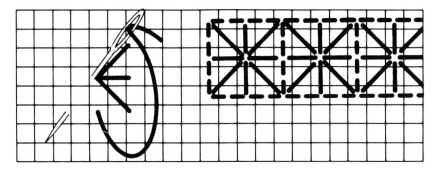

Algerian Eye stitch (back stitching used to close gaps around stitches)

Ribbons pincushion.

RIBBONS PINCUSHION

Two of the canvas work projects for this chapter act as samplers; they use a selection of stitches which are laid with coloured ribbons to great effect.

MATERIALS

Anchor Pearl Cotton No 5 in 5g skeins;
White 01 ⎫
Grey 0397 ⎬   1 skein each
Grey 0398 ⎭
6 in (15 cm) square single thread tapestry canvas, 18 threads to the inch (2.5 cm).
6 in (15 cm) square matching velvet or other fabric for backing
1¼ yd (1.2 m) 3 mm wide double face satin ribbon (Offray 012 Silver)
½ yd (40 cm) fine matching cord for trimming.
Stuffing; kapok, sawdust, bran, polyester/acrylic stuffing or cotton wool as available.
Tapestry needle, size 20.

The layout diagram gives the complete design, centre indicated by broken lines which should coincide with the tacking stitches. Follow the layout diagram to complete the design.

DIAGRAM 1

1 — 01 ⎫ Satin stitch
2 — 0397 ⎭

3 — 0397 ⎫ Petit Point stitch   ⎬ Chequer stitch
4 — 0398 ⎭

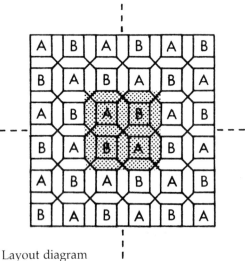

Layout diagram

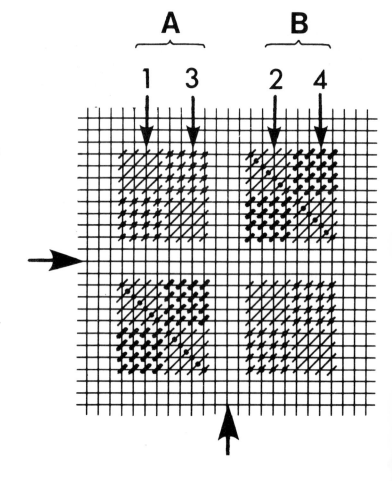

TO WORK

1.   Mark the centre thread of canvas lengthwise and widthwise with a line of tacking stitches. Bind the edges of the canvas if required with masking thread to stop fraying and cotton catching as you work.

2.   Commence the design centrally, following the charts given. Diagram 1 gives a complete section of the design, centre indicated by large black arrows which should coincide with the tacking stitches. It also shows the arrangement of stitches on the threads of canvas represented by the background lines. The shaded area shows the central section in diagram 1.

Diagram 2 shows the stitches used to get the chequered effect. Alternating squares of Petit Point stitch (tent stitch worked on fine canvas – – Gros Point is tent stitch worked on a coarser canvas) and Satin stitch are used, worked over four horizontal and four vertical threads of canvas.

Chequer stitch consists of alternating squares of Petit Point stitch and Satin stitch, worked over four horizontal and four vertical threads of canvas.

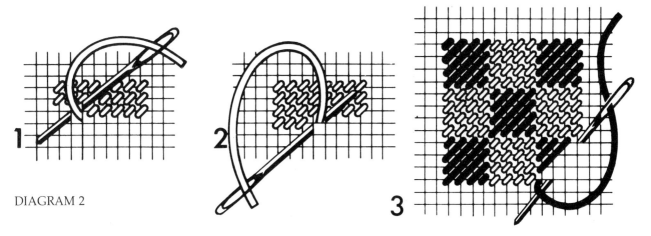

DIAGRAM 2

The easiest method of working is to work the squares in diagonal rows starting at the upper left hand corner. To work Petit Point stitch, the rows are worked from right to left and vice versa. The Satin stitch squares are worked diagonally across the canvas threads.

3.   When the embroidery is finished, trim the canvas to within ¾″ (1.5 cm) on all sides.

4.   Cut the ribbon into ten equal lengths. Lay each length between the vertical and horizontal spaces left between the motifs and pin in position to secure. Work a cross stitch in 0398 across the ribbons and through the canvas (over 3 × 3 threads) at each intersection. (See Diagram 3).

5.   To make up, trim velvet or backing fabric to same size as canvas. Place right sides together and pin and tack. Stitch together close to embroidery, leaving an opening on one side for stuffing.

Bring the thread through at the lower right hand side of the ribbon intersection and insert at the upper left hand side, forming a half cross. To complete, bring the needle through at the lower left hand side and insert at the upper right hand side.

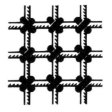

DIAGRAM 3

MAKING A TWISTED CORD
With two people, using pencils or knitting needles, loop the thread for the decorative cord around the pencil or needle several times (the loop must be about three times the length of the finished cord and about half the required finished thickness). Twist the pencils or needles round and round in opposite directions until the cord starts forming kinks. Holding the cord in the middle, let the two halves spiral together. Knot tightly at the pencil end and remove the pencils.

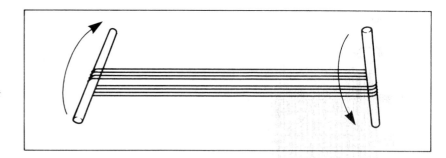

6.   Turn right side out, stuff firmly and slip stitch open edges together. Sew cord round.

This project works beautifully in other colours to fit any colour scheme.

RIBBONS CUSHION

This cushion also uses laid-on ribbon but has a greater selection of stitches to practice. All the embroidery is worked before the ribbons are added. Use the suggested colours or match your own decor.

Ribbons cushion.

MATERIALS

Anchor Tapisserie Wool (10 m skeins);
Saxe Blue 0144 (6 skeins)
Peach 0366 (5 skeins)
Petrol Blue 0848 (5 skeins)
Haze 0705 (4 skeins)
White 0402 (1 skein)
Anchor Stranded Cotton;
Kingfisher 0161 (1 skein) Use 3 strands throughout.
16 in (40 cm) single thread tapestry canvas, 16 threads to the inch (2.5 cm), 27 in wide (69 cm).
16 in (40 cm) matching medium weight fabric for backing, 36 in (90 cm) wide.
1¾ yd (1.70 cm) French Blue velvet ribbon, ⅜ in (9 mm) wide (Offray 4011).
1½ yd (1.40 m) matching cord
Cushion pad to fit
Tapestry frame with 27 in (68 cm) tapes
Size 18 tapestry needle for wool, size 24 for cotton.

TO WORK

1.   Mark the centre of the canvas lengthwise and widthwise with a line of tacking stitches. Mount the canvas on the frame with the long edges to the tapes.

DIAGRAM 1

The threads of the canvas are represented by the background lines on the diagram.

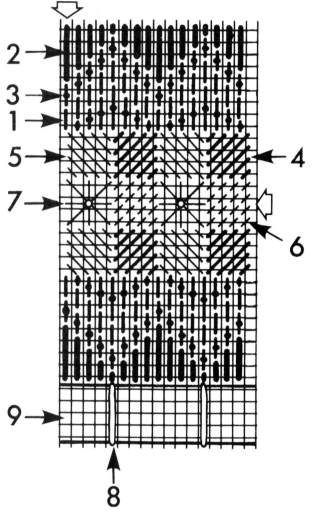

2 →
3 →
1 →
5 →
7 →
9 →

→ 4

6

8

1 — 0144 ⎫
2 — 0705 ⎬ Vertical Satin
3 — 0848 ⎭ stitch

4 — 0144 ⎫ Diagonal Satin
5 — 0366 ⎬ stitch

6 — 0366 Petit Point stitch
7 — 0402 Double cross stitch
8 — 0161 Straight stitch
9 — Ribbon

Double Cross stitch. This is worked over four horizontal and vertical threads. When working this stitch, the last upper stitch of each should lie in the same direction throughout.

DIAGRAM 2

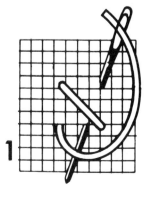

1

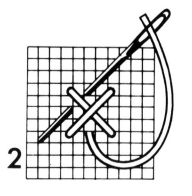

2

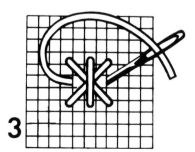

3

DIAGRAM 3

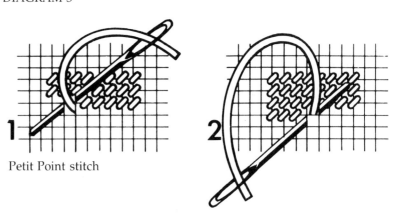

Petit Point stitch

2.   Start work centrally. Follow diagram 1 and number key for the embroidery. The arrows on the diagram show the centre of the design and should coincide with the tacking stitches. Work all the embroidery before attaching the ribbons.

3.   The section given in diagram 1 is worked six more times to the right and seven times to the left. Work four more bands of embroidery in the same way; two above and two below the centre.

4.   When the embroidery is completed, cut the ribbon into four equal lengths. Lay a length of ribbon into each space left between the bands of embroidery. Pin in position to secure and using three strands of 0161, work a straight stitch across the ribbon and through the canvas. Work a stitch every eight threads.

5.   Trim canvas and ribbon to within $\frac{3}{4}$ in (1.5 cm) on all sides. Cut a piece of backing fabric the same size. Place right sides together and stitch together, close to embroidery. Leave a short side open for inserting the cushion pad.

6.   Turn right side out and insert pad. Slip stitch the open edges together and sew cord round.

FLORENTINE CUSHION

MATERIALS

Anchor Stranded Cotton; use 6 strands throughout:

Forest Green 0213	5 skeins
Jade 0189	2 skeins
Jade 0187	1 skein
Apple Green 0205	1 skein
Laurel Green 0212	1 skein

Forest Green 0215   1 skein;
Emerald 0226   1 skein;
       0227   1 skein
Parrot Green 0257   1 skein;
30 cm single thread tapestry canvas 22 threads (21 holes) to 2.5 cm, 58 cm wide.
40 cm matching medium weight fabric 91 cm wide for front and back.
Cushion pad to fit.
Tapestry frame.
Milward International Range tapestry needle No. 20.

Florentine cushion.

KEY TO DIAGRAM

— 0187   FOUNDATION ROW

2 — 0226
3 — 0257
4 — 0227
5 — 0189
6 — 0212
7 — 0213
8 — 0205
9 — 0215

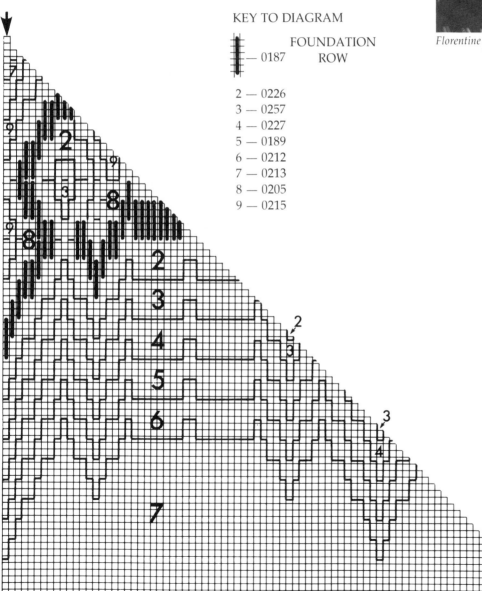

TO WORK

1.   Cut a piece from canvas 30 × 30 cm and mark the centre both ways with a line of basting stitches. Diagram 1 gives one eighth of the complete design, centre indicated by black arrows which should coincide with the basting stitches. Diagram 1 also shows the arrangement of the stitches on the threads of the canvas represented by the background lines.

2.   The design is worked throughout in Florentine Stitch over 6 canvas threads, but it will be necessary to adjust the length of stitches to fit the diagonal corners and give a neat outer edge. Commence the design centrally and work the foundation row 48 threads down from crossed basting stitches following diagram 1 and key to diagram.

3.   Following pattern, work each numbered section in the appropriate colour, taking care to fill in area 7 in 0213 only, following the stitch sequence. To complete one side, work the given eighth in reverse from the lengthwise basting stitches.

4.   Turn canvas and work other three sides in the same way.

5.   On completion of embroidery trim canvas to within 1.5 cm of embroidery. Cut two pieces from fabric 40 cm × 40 cm. Place the embroidery centrally to one piece of fabric and mark the outline of the finished edge of the embroidery with a line of basting stitches.

6.   Cut out centre section of fabric to within 1.5 cm of basting stitches, clipping fabric diagonally at the corners to the basting stitches. Fold back fabric at centre to the wrong side, place on top of embroidery and baste and edge stitch.

7.   Place back and front right sides together, baste and stitch 1.5 cm from edge on all sides leaving an opening on one side for pad insertion. Turn to right side, insert pad and sew open edges.

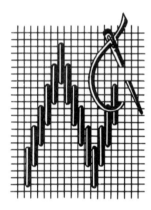

Diagram 2. Florentine Stitch. This stitch is used for working zig-zag patterns known as Florentine Work It is generally used to fill a large area and is then worked in two or more rows of different colours forming an all over wave pattern. The diagram shows the method of working a single row of stitches over 6 threads.

CHAPTER SEVEN

FREESTYLE EMBROIDERY

Freestyle or freehand embroidery has a freedom and fluidity that makes it suitable for almost any project and its adaptability means you can experiment to get a wide variety of results.

The 'free' from the name of this group of stitches comes from the lack of restriction in working; it isn't necessary to count threads or work over a canvas mesh and the grain of the fabric needn't be followed. Although the formation of the stitch may be shared with that of more controlled work, freehand stitches can be worked as an outline if worked apart, as a filling if worked closely or regularly to give an even pattern. Flowing lines are easy to achieve.

This group of stitches is probably the largest there is within the many types of embroidery and the stitches have been used over the centuries — the methods of working have hardly changed over the years. Some stitches are characteristic of particular countries and may be known by a country's name, like Cretan stitch or Romanian stitch.

CHOOSING FABRIC

Freestyle embroidery can be worked on almost any fabric. The conventional fabrics are linens and cottons, which are obtainable in a wide variety of weights and qualities — some fine fabric may cost ten times the cheapest. Pure cotton and linen is widely available but for projects that may need regular laundering, a mix like polyester cotton may be suitable. Look for the Zweigart range of fabric for good choice in weights and colours.

Although there is a good selection of purpose-made embroidery fabric,

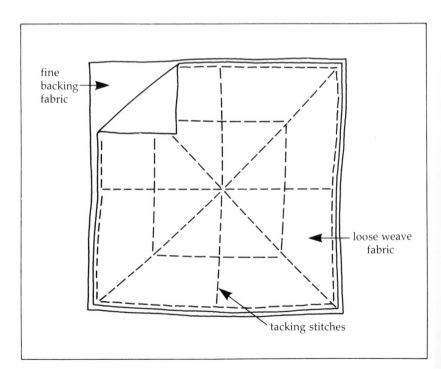

Tack a backing fabric to very loose weave material. It can then be used for embroidery.

don't neglect other sources. Dressmaking and furnishing fabric will include a far wider colour range and may offer some useful effects for you to exploit, like embroidery around a regular motif.

Very loose weave fabrics can be used but aren't always easy to work. Tack a backing fabric on the wrong side if necessary, make sure that both fabrics are well secured together. Work the stitches through both layers for stability.

There is no reason why you can't use even weave fabric intended for counted work for freestyle embroidery, but remember that even weave can be more expensive than the equivalent plain weave.

As freestyle stitchery lends itself to experimentation, you can also experiment with the ground fabric. Builder's scrim can be used for eyecatching bold work. If you use very fine fabric, be careful about passing threads over the back and finishing off as it may show through.

CHOOSING THREAD

As in most other cases, choosing thread is integral to considering the design. Use a thread that is smooth enough to pass through the material easily and balance the weight of the thread with the embroidery fabric. Generally speaking, fine fabrics need fine threads and so on, but mix weights for texture and special effects. Textured threads are difficult to use as they have to pass through the woven fabric and may be better laid on and sewn over ('couched').

Consider the thickness of the thread in relation to the planned stitches and the size of the stitch.

Crewel needles are most suitable for this type of work although a chenille needle can be used for thick threads. Use a blunt tapestry needle if a second stitch is worked between the first — this will stop the first layer of threads being split by a pointed needle.

Most types of thread can be used for freestyle work, depending on the scale and textures required. A type of freestyle embroidery that uses crewel wool alone is called, not surprisingly, crewel work or sometimes, Jacobean work. The second name comes from the period in which it was popularised.

Designs are usually traditional to this time too, when large hangings were in fashion in the late seventeenth and early eighteenth centuries. The designs were large and were often based on a tree or other natural forms.

The attraction of crewel work lies in the many fine stitches that lie on the surface of the material, each stitch carefully laid to cover the motif. As crewel wool is fine and comes in a wide range of colours, very subtle shading and details can be obtained.

For working crewel, the fabric needs to be firm to bear the weight of the wool, as it is closely set and can cover large areas. The work was originally designed for heavy furnishing items, but it is unusual to see it on such a large scale today, where it is most often worked for items like cushions and some decorative items. As quite long stitches are worked, it is not suitable for items where the threads could be caught and pulled.

A traditional crewel design

DESIGNS

It is almost impossible to give design suggestions for freestyle embroidery as the possibilities are so great. Almost any design that can be drawn can be sewn using freestyle techniques. Apart from the traditional pictures or cushions, freestyle techniques can be used on boxes made from fabric, accessories like belts, bags and fashion items, small gifts and objects, furnishings like lamp bases and curtain tie backs, wallhangings, and household linen.

Commercial transfers are almost always intended for freestyle embroidery and the clear, defined lines that make up a commercial design are easy to copy when you design for yourself. A strong design, that can be simply drawn, needn't be a plain design when worked, as the vast possibilities of the different stitches can transform it into an intricate piece, full of texture and colour.

Because of the variety, freestyle stitches are very good for working abstract pieces that rely on thread and colour for its impact. They are also good for working samplers and this is an ideal way for beginners to start, as they have a record and example of the stitches they have worked.

WORKING STITCHES

Like all other types of embroidery, freestyle stitches need to be evenly worked and lie flat on the fabric surface. The right tension is very important for a good finished result — too tight and the fabric will pucker, too loose and the stitches won't lie flat.

Look at your design carefully before you start. Which parts are underneath or lower than others? Work these first to give a realistic effect. For looped stitches bring the needle up before the thread is pulled through and use your free hand to guide the loop around the needle.

When following design lines on the embroidery fabric, work to the outside of the design, making sure that the lines are covered by the stitching — not all transfer lines wash out.

Choose your stitches to mirror or copy the effect you wish to create — fine, feathery stitches will be good for birds, some flowers and will make natural-looking leaves. Stitches can either be used to outline a shape or to fill it in — if filled in it may be that no fabric can show through; or more open stitches for a textured effect. Some stitches will be more suitable for each purpose than others.

If working to a chart, either your own or a commercial one, allow space for your own interpretation. Neither are absolute and your own touches will make the effect that bit more special.

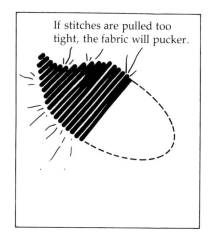

If stitches are pulled too tight, the fabric will pucker.

STITCH DIRECTORY

FREESTYLE EMBROIDERY

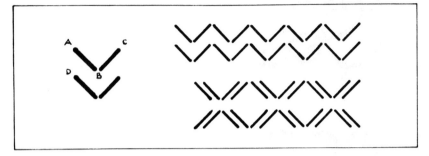

Arrowhead stitch

Basic backstitch is worked by bringing the needle out a stitch length away along the design line from the end of the last stitch. The needle is re-inserted close to the end of the last stitch.

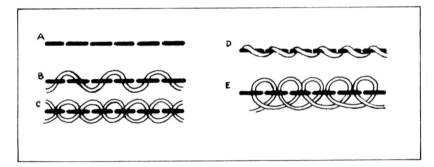

Backstitch and variations

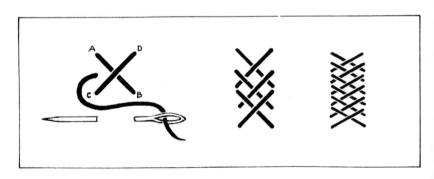

Basket stitch

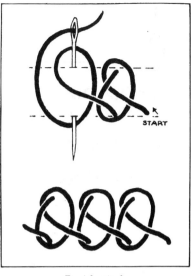

Braid stitch

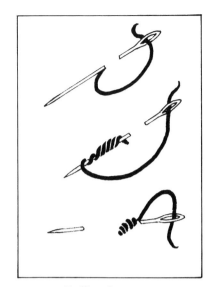

Bullion knot

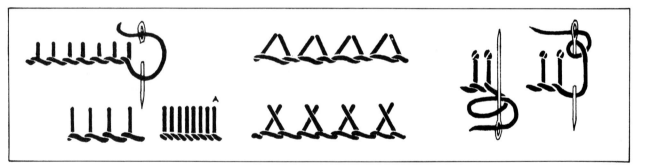

Blanket stitch and variations
(A) is buttonhole stitch

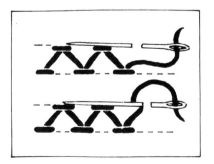

Chevron stitch

Coral stitch

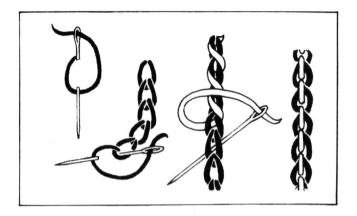

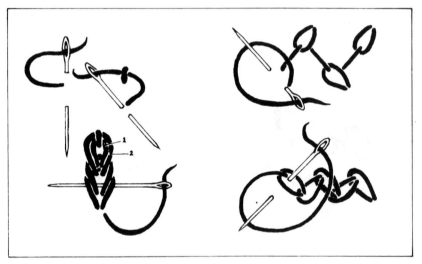

Chain stitch and variations

Cretan stitch closed and open

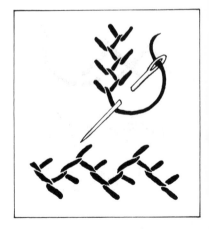

Feather stitch

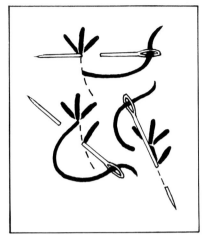

Fern stitch

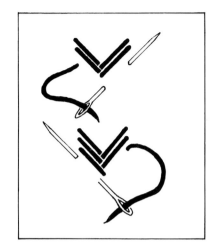

Fishbone stitch

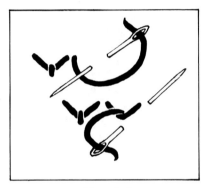

Fly stitch

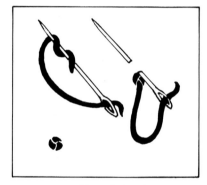

French knot

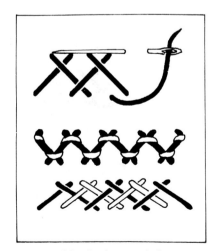

Herringbone stitch

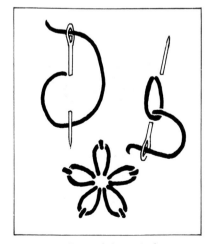

Lazy daisy stitch

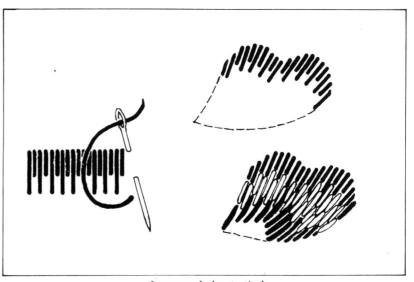

Long and short stitch
(all rows following foundation row use stitches of the same length)

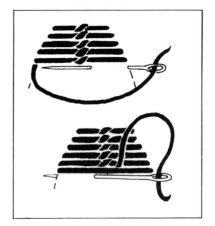

Roman stitch

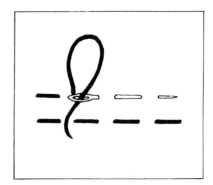

Running stitch

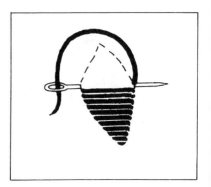

Satin stitch

Seeding stitch

Sheaf stitch

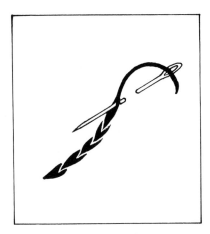

Split stitch

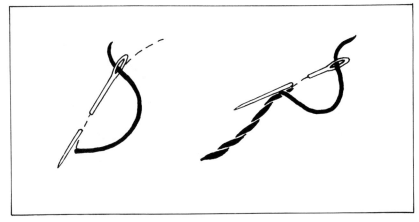

Stem stitch

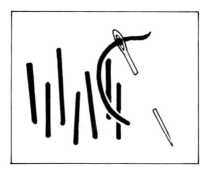

Straight stitch

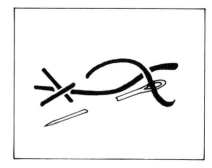

Thorn stitch

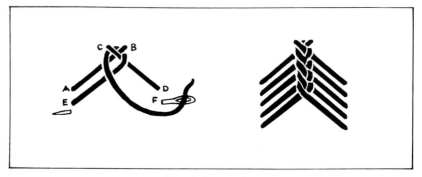

Vandyke stitch

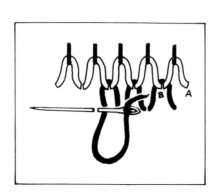

Wave stitch

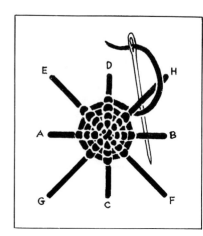

Woven web

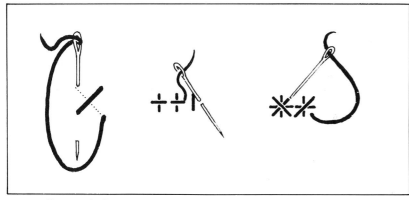

Cross-stitch   Upright cross-stitch   Double cross-stitch

DESERT ISLAND DREAM

This easily and quickly worked cushion has great effect and uses two different background colours to create the desert island.

DIAGRAM 1

The diagram is reversed for the image in the water. You can trace directly from this drawing as it is full size.

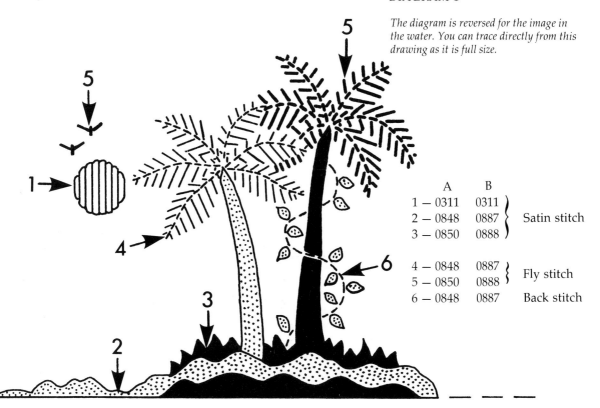

	A	B	
1 —	0311	0311	}
2 —	0848	0887	} Satin stitch
3 —	0850	0888	}
4 —	0848	0887	}
5 —	0850	0888	} Fly stitch
6 —	0848	0887	Back stitch

Anchor Stranded Cotton, 1 skein each:
Tangerine 0311;
Marine Blue 0848 and 0850;
Caramel 0887 and 0888;
(use three strands throughout).
$\frac{1}{2}$ yd (50 cm) blue fine weight fabric, 36 in (90 cm) wide.
$\frac{1}{3}$ yd (30 cm) cream fine weight fabric 36 in (90 cm) wide.
1 $\frac{3}{4}$ yd (1.6 m) matching cord.
Cushion pad to fit.
No. 7 crewel needle.

Fly stitch. Bring the thread through at the top left, hold it down with the left thumb, insert the needle to the right on the same level a little distance from where the thread first emerged and take a small stitch downwards to the centre with the thread below the needle. Pull through and insert the needle again below the stitch at the centre and bring it through in position for the next stitch.

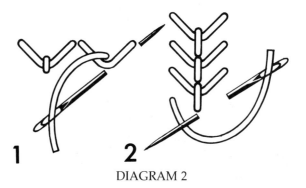

DIAGRAM 2

TO MAKE

1. Cut a piece 17 in × 9 in from each fabric and place right sides together with raw edges even. Pin, tack and stitch $\frac{3}{4}$ in (1.5 cm) from one long edge. Press seam flat.

2. Transfer the design from the full size drawing onto the right side of the fabric, 3 in (8 cm) in from the right hand side. The dotted line shows the centre of the design, which is repeated, upside down on the blue fabric.

3. Work the embroidery following the diagram and the key, following key A for the cream fabric and key B for the blue. All parts similar to the numbered parts are worked in the same colour and stitch.

4. When the embroidery is completed, press on the wrong side.

5. Cut a backing piece the same size from the remaining blue fabric for back. Place right sides together with front and stitch $\frac{3}{4}$ in (1.5 cm) from edge around three sides, leaving one side open.

6. Insert pad through open side and slip stitch closed. Sew cord in position around all edges.

FLORAL FANTASY

The directions for this cushion use stranded cotton and a fine weight fabric, but the motif has such universal appeal it is easily adapted. Use the same dimensions and working instructions but try crewel wool on a slightly heavier fabric. Use freestyle stitches as suggested or fill in the design with satin stitch and similar filling stitches to get the effect of crewel work — the motif has a lot in common with the traditional Jacobean designs.

MATERIALS

Anchor stranded cotton; 3 skeins White 01.
½ yd (50 cm) grey fine weight fabric 36 in (90 cm) wide.
1½ yd (1.50 cm) no. 2 piping cord.
1 card Coats bias binding, white, for covering piping cord.
Cushion pad to fit.

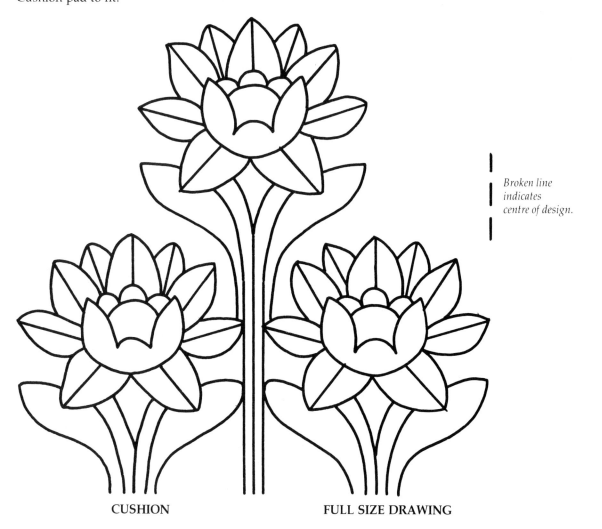

Broken line indicates centre of design.

CUSHION   **FULL SIZE DRAWING**

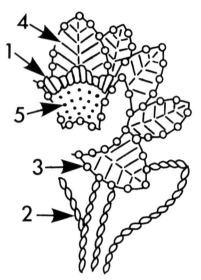

All parts similar to the number parts are worked in the same stitch.

1 Satin stitch
2 Stem stitch
3 Mountmellick stitch
4 Fern stitch
5 French knot

Mountmellick stitch. Bring the thread through at A, insert at B and bring out at C. Pass the needle under the diagonal stitch just made without piercing the fabric. Pull the thread through and re-insert the needle at A, bring out again at C keeping the thread under the needle point. Insert the needle at D and bring through at E. Pass the needle under the diagonal stitch just made. To complete the second stitch, insert the needle again at C and bring out again at E.

French Knots. Bring the thread out at the required position, hold the thread down with the left thumb and encircle the thread twice with the needle. Still holding the thread, twist the needle back to the starting point and insert close to where the thread first emerged. Pull thread to the back and secure or pass on to the next stitch.

TO MAKE

1.   Cut a piece of fabric 18 in × 13½ in (45 cm × 34 cm). Finish edges if required to prevent fraying. Fold in half widthwise and crease lightly along the fold.

2.   With one long side of the fabric facing, trace the design given onto the left side half of the fabric, 2 in (5.5 cm) from the lower edge. The drawing gives half the design for the cushion. The centre is indicated by the broken lines which should coincide with the fold. To complete, trace the design again on to the right half of the fabric.

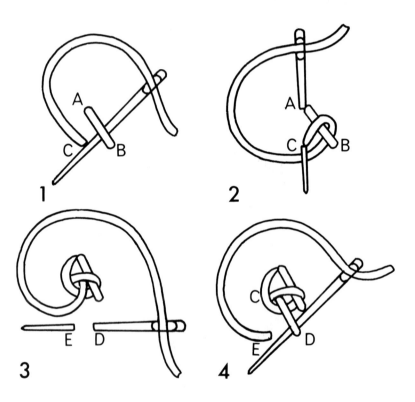

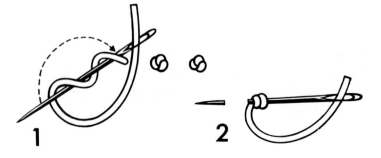

3. Work the embroidery following diagram 1 and the key to the diagram. Three strands of thread are used throughout.

4. When the embroidery is complete, press on the wrong side or block into shape if required.

5. Cut a piece of fabric for backing to the same dimensions as the front. Cover piping cord with bias binding and place to right side of the front, raw edges even and joining ends to fit.

6. Pin, tack and stitch front to back with right sides together close to piping cord. Leave an opening to insert the cushion pad.

7. Insert pad and slip stitch opening together.

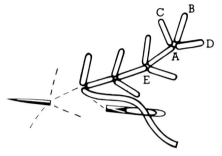

Fern stitch. Bring the needle through at A and make a straight stitch to B. Bring the thread through again at A and make another straight stitch to C. Repeat once more at D and bring the thread through at E to commence the next three radiating stitches. The central stitch follows the line of the design.

Desert Island Dream

Floral Fantasy

CHAPTER EIGHT

COUNTED CROSS STITCH

Much of the current popularity of counted cross stitch comes from America where the technique has gone through a recent revival — resulting in some very original new designs and a market dealing in accessories for cross stitchers only.

However, cross stitch has a long and honourable history with its roots in Europe, particularly the East. It has been used to decorate peasant costume for centuries and was usually worked in bright colours with motifs varying from native shapes to intricate designs. It has also been used for rugs and areas that need to stand hard wear as the whole background fabric can be covered if required.

Today it is used for a wide variety of work. In some designs, its early origins show, particularly from Scandinavia where there is a strong cross stitch tradition in picturing floral motifs. As cross stitch can be worked on almost any scale, it is suitable for canvas work as well as on linen or other fabrics.

There are several variations on the basic cross stitch which are usually worked on canvas or coarser fabrics — designs intended to be worked in cross stitch on a light or medium weight fabric are usually completed in the one stitch. More may be combined for more modern work or projects on a larger or coarser scale. Cross stitch can also be combined with other counted stitches.

CHOOSING FABRIC

Cross stitch relies on regularity for its effect, so you should choose a fabric that will give an exactly square stitch of regular size. For this reason, cross stitch is best worked on even weave fabric, where there are the same number of threads horizontally and vertically. Canvas and rug canvas fit into this category, as do even weave linens, cottons and mixes where the threads can be evenly counted. Most embroidery shops stock a range of fabrics that are even weave, varying between 14–36 threads to the inch (2.5 cm). These are also available in a range of colours to suit individual projects.

Hardanger fabric and Aida are specialist fabrics particularly suitable for cross stitch as the threads are woven in pairs or fours to form blocks that give a basketweave effect. This fabric is very easy to sew as stitches are formed over each block without having to count threads.

You can work cross stitch on plain weave fabric, but it is less easy to achieve the regular effect that is characteristic of cross stitch. There are also some commercial transfer patterns that can be ironed onto plain weave. Fabrics like gingham, where the woven pattern of blocks can be followed, can also be used.

It is also possible to work a cross stitch design, using the 'waste canvas' method.

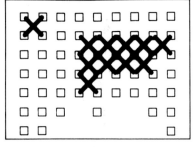

Aida, Binca and Hardanger fabrics are woven with a network of regular holes that make it easy to locate stitches.

CHOOSING THREAD

Stranded cotton, and the finer threads like coton perle are usually used with most medium weight fabrics, but threads can be matched to most fabrics to get the right result; wool on hessian, soft embroidery cotton on loose weave fabrics etc. Danish flower thread, a specialist thread imported from Denmark in natural, subtle flower and plant colours is also available in embroidery stores. This is a thin natural thread which works very well on fine fabrics and is used especially for depicting flora and fauna.

Rug wool can also be used on canvas for rugs and the range of embroidery wools is used to cover canvas with cross stitch — you must ensure that all the canvas is covered as you sew.

As you are working into the holes in a fabric or canvas, use a tapestry needle best suited to the thread. If working on plain weave fabric, you will need a needle with a point to pierce the fabric. A crewel needle is suitable.

DESIGNING

All designing for cross stitch is best done on graph paper (available from stationery stores or office suppliers) as each block on the graph corresponds to one complete cross stitch. This duplicates the way that professional charts and designs are presented and is by far the easiest way to read and copy a design. Although it is possible with much work to create very subtle designs, the graphic nature of the finished stitches lend themselves to more simplified shapes and motifs — the subtle shading and shapes possible with freestyle embroidery, for instance, are difficult to duplicate with cross stitch.

As the stitches are also rather angular it isn't possible to get flowing lines but these difficulties are overcome by the charm that cross stitch has in rendering shapes into simple forms.

When planning your own designs, it helps to work out colours by using coloured pencils etc. to colour the blocks as the design develops. If you are trying to chart a design from another source, use tracing paper with a graph grid printed on it — it's then an easy job to square the design on the tracing paper on top of the design you wish to copy.

Cross stitch is particularly suitable for folk motifs and abstract designs that can be combined or used in isolation to create a number of effects. They can be used on household linen (place mats, tablecloths etc.) but cross stitch designs are suitable for pictures, cushions and for inserting panels into clothing and accessories.

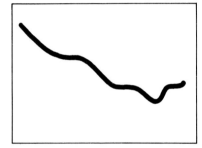

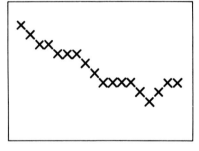

Perfect flowing lines are not easy to work with angular cross-stitch, but using a tracing paper graph over the lines to be stitched will let you chart the line as well as possible.

ASSISI WORK

This type of specialist cross stitch technique originated in Italy in a town called Assisi in the fifteenth or sixteenth century. Assisi work uses geometric designs and two stitches; cross stitch and Holbein or double running stitch.

The motif is outlined with Holbein stitch and the background worked in cross stitch using black, red or dark blue — leaving the motif in white or cream (depending on the colour of the background fabric). More modern

Assisi work reverses the traditional rules of cross stitch — the motif or design is left unstitched and the background is worked to define the shape required. Holbein stitch is used to outline the design.

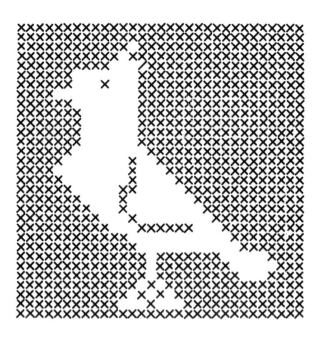

pieces use perhaps a darker background fabric and green or orange for the cross stitch but the tradition is the same.

WASTE CANVAS

It is possible to work cross stitch on a fabric that is otherwise unsuitable by using waste canvas.

To use this technique, choose a single plain canvas that suits the thread thickness you want to use and the finished stitch size you require. Cut a piece about two inches bigger all round than the design you wish to sew. Tack the canvas onto the fabric in the position you want your embroidery. Work the embroidery using the canvas as a guide for the stitches, using one mesh of the canvas to one stitch. When the work is complete, use a clean sponge to damp the canvas and leave for a few minutes. Undo the tacking and, using a pair of tweezers, gently pull away the canvas thread by thread, leaving the embroidery behind.

WORKING CROSS STITCH

Regular, even stitches are the basic ingredient of successful cross stitch. Choosing the right fabric will help, as will working on a hoop.

There are two schools of thought about working cross stitch — one says that each stitch should be completed before going on to the next one whilst the other maintains that blocks of one colour are easier to work if you work the lower stitch in a row and go back with the upper stitch in a row. You will find which one is best for you but the one essential to observe, whichever you choose, is that all the top stitches should lie in the same direction. If they lie at different angles, the light will catch differently and the wrong ones will stand out like a sore thumb.

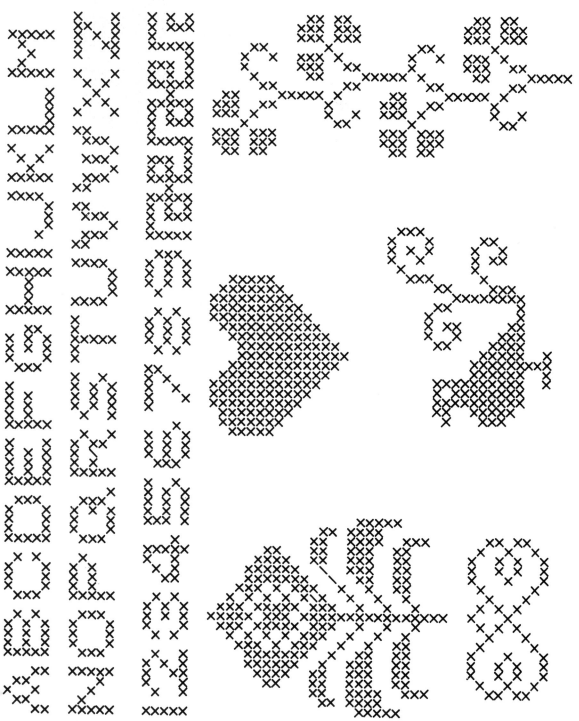

*These motifs and alphabet are easily
combined to make a sampler.*

One of the best ways of practising cross stitch is to work a sampler. These emulate the charming examples worked in bygone days and lend themselves to the folk or native motifs that suit cross stitch so well. A selection of motifs and alphabets are included for you to design and work a simple sampler.

STITCH DIRECTORY

COUNTED CROSS STITCH

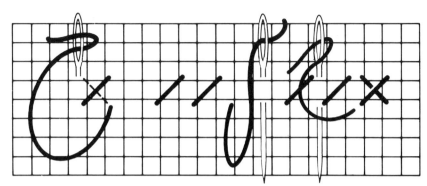

Basic cross stitch can be worked one complete stitch at a time, or worked in lower and upper rows.

Cross stitch variations
(these stitches are not suitable for working commercial charts intended for 'square' stitches)

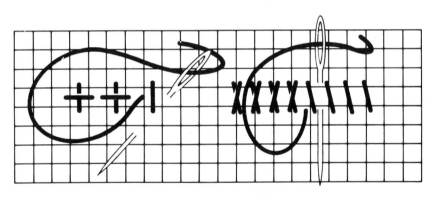

Upright cross stitch   Oblong cross stitch

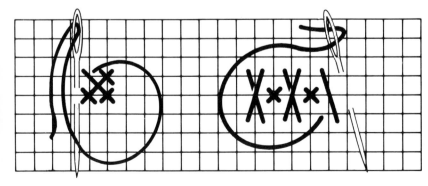

Rice stitch   Double stitch

OUR TOWN

This charming cross stitch 'town' uses subtle colour to give an harmonious and peaceful picture that could fit into almost any room. Alter the colours for your own scheme if you want, perhaps altering the background colour too. The instructions call for evenweave linen but you could also work the design on 11 blocks to the inch (2.5 cm). Aida — the finished piece will be a very similar size.

KEY TO DIAGRAM

⊡ — 02

■ — 0358

1 ⊟ — 0392   4 ⊙ — 0882

2 ⊠ — 0779   5 ⊙ — 0884

3 ☑ — 0849   6 Ⲧ — 0942

MATERIALS

Anchor Stranded Cotton; use 3 strands throughout:

Peat Brown 0358   2 skeins
Cream 02   1 skein
Linen 0392   1 skein

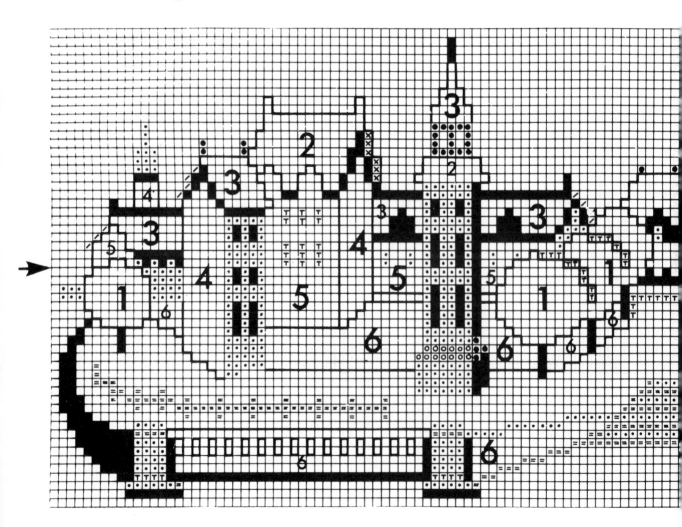

Marine Blue 0779, 0849 ⎫
Flesh Pink 0882, 0884 ⎬ 1 skein each
Maize 0942   ⎭
12 in (30 cm) natural even weave embroidery fabric, 29 threads to the inch
(2.5 cm).
Size 24 tapestry needle.
Purchased frame to fit (best bought on completion).

TO MAKE

1. Mark the centre of the fabric lengthwise and widthwise. Use tacking
stitches or use a blue marking pen. Bind the edges of the fabric to prevent
fraying as you work.

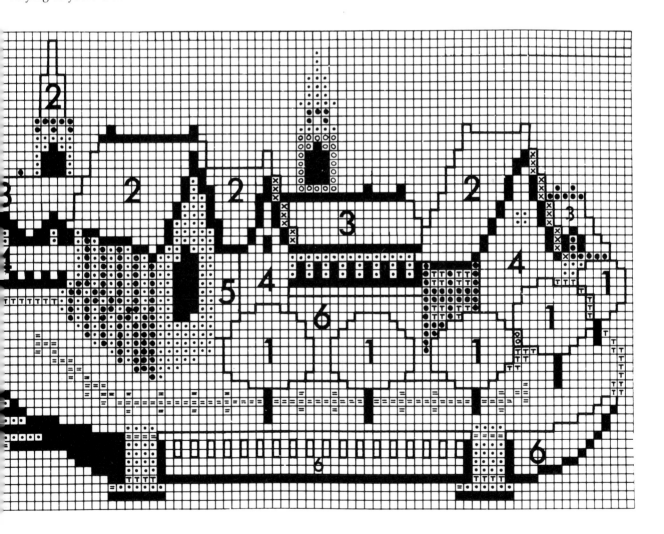

2.   The diagram gives the complete design, with the centre indicated by the black arrows, which should coincide with the centre marking on the fabric. Each square on the chart corresponds to three fabric threads or one cross stitch. Each cross stich is worked over three threads and it is important that the upper half of the crosses should lie in the same direction throughout.

3.   Commence the design centrally, with a long side of the fabric facing. Follow the chart for stitch placement and the colour key.

4.   When the embroidery is complete, press the embroidery on the wrong side.

5.   Following manufacturer's instructions, place the picture in the frame. See also the chapter on finishing.

DAMASK TABLECLOTH

MATERIALS

Anchor Stranded Cotton; use 3 strands throughout:
Kingfisher 0159   3 skeins
Muscat Green 0280   3 skeins
Gorse Yellow 0301   3 skeins
Cobalt Blue 0130   2 skeins
Gorse Yellow 0303   2 skeins
Hyacinth 0940   2 skeins
Zweigart "Delos" damask embroidery fabric, 100% cotton, 1908/253 (ecru) 140 cm wide: 5 × 5 embroidery circles (see layout diagram).
Milward International Range tapestry needle No. 24.

TO MAKE

1.   Mark the centre block of each circle to be embroidered (see heavy black circles on layout) lengthwise and widthwise with a line of tacking stitches. Diagram 1 gives the complete circular design, the black arrows indicate the centre and should coincide with the blasting stitches. Each background square on the diagram represents one block, one cross stitch or straight stitch.

2.   Work the embroidery following diagram 1 and sign key.

3.   On completion, press embroidery on the wrong side.

4.   To make up, turn back 2.5 cm hems, mitre corners and stitch in position.

KEY TO DIAGRAM

☒	0130
⊡	0159
▣	0280
▤	0301
◉	0303
■	0940
▨	0940 — Straight stitch

}Cross stitch

DELOS FABRIC CUTTING AND
EMBROIDERY LAY-OUT (NOT TO SCALE)

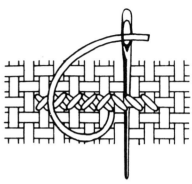

Diagram 2. Cross Stitch. Bring the needle
through at the lower right hand side,
insert the needle 1 block up and 1 block to
the left and bring out 1 block down, thus
forming a half cross, continue in this way
to the end of the row. Complete the upper
half of the cross as shown. Cross Stitch
may be worked from right to left or left to
right but it is important that the upper
half of all crosses should lie in the same
direction.

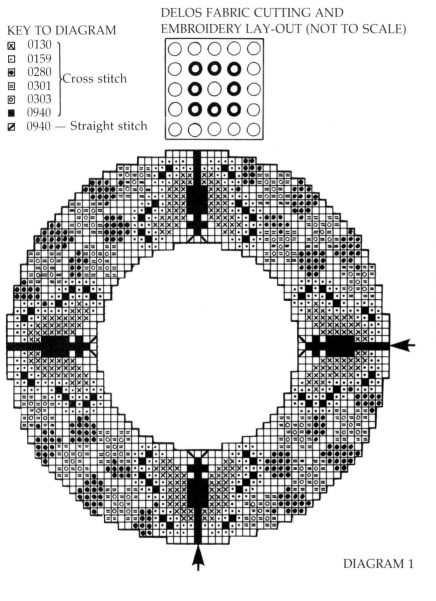

DIAGRAM 1

CHAPTER NINE

CUTWORK

Cutwork is a delightful form of embroidery that really falls into the 'openwork' category but deserves special consideration on its own. It is an old and traditional type of embroidery that became fashionable in the sixteenth century but is still worked widely today.

Traditionally, it was done on white or natural coloured linen in a white or natural thread. It looks very difficult but, in fact, uses only a few stitches to outline the design. The fabric portions in between the design are then cut away, leaving a delicate, lacy look.

Nowadays, coloured thread and fabric can be used, especially if the work is done for table linen or on clothing. If large cut away areas are required, like in table linen, they can be reinforced with embroidered bars that bridge the open area. Some surface or freestyle stitches can be added to enhance the design.

CHOOSING FABRIC

Closely woven fabrics that are not likely to fray are suitable for cut work and as well as the traditional linen, fabrics like Viyella and organdie are suitable.

CHOOSING THREAD

Coton à broder, pearl cotton or stranded cotton can all be used successfully for cutwork on medium weight fabric. Thinner threads like machine embroidery cotton can be used on fine fabrics. If you are going for a less traditional look, strands of crewel wool, Persian wool or tapestry wool can be used on thicker fabrics, especially for garments. Use a crewel needle of the right size for the thread.

DESIGNS

Because of the technique of cutting away fabric, there are some restrictions on the types of designs that are suitable for cutwork. Generally floral designs are used, but geometric shapes work well as borders. Transfers are available for cut work and can be adapted — a design for a tray cloth, for example, can easily be used on a table cloth with the borders extended.

If you are designing your own motif or pattern, the best way of working is to regard the design as a positive and negative — the cut away area is the negative. Colour your drawing or design, using the same colour for all the cut away areas. Follow this carefully — once fabric is cut, the material cannot be repaired and the embroidery will be difficult to save.

You can approach your design in different ways; you can treat it like a stencil where all the main sections are cut away; you can leave the motif alone and cut away the background, leaving the motif as a silhouette; the third way is to leave some of the main motif whole with small, interior sections cut away.

This last approach is used to get the shaped edge that is characteristic of cut work and allows a design to be positioned at the outer edge of the fabric.

CHOOSING STITCHES AND WORKING THE DESIGN

The two main stitches for cut work are buttonhole stitch with some variations and running stitch.

Most cut work motifs are presented as double lines outlining the design. The running stitches are used to go around the outline, just within the lines of the design. The ridge of running stitches strengthens the edge and pads it slightly to raise the embroidery. Your work should be mounted in a frame to keep it even and neat. Stitches should be small and even and not pulled as this will twist and pucker the work.

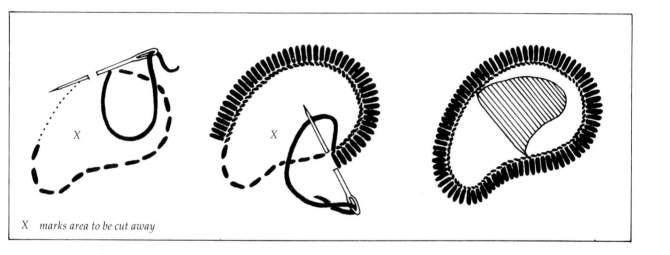

X marks area to be cut away

Buttonhole stitch is then used to cover the running stitches, working from left to right (right to left if you are left handed). The needle should be inserted into the material on the inside of the design so that the ridge of the stitch is facing the area to be cut away.

Double buttonhole stitch can also be worked and there are variations on the basic stitch to be found in this chapter. All stitches should be worked as close together as possible.

When all the embroidery is done, the areas that are to cut out should be marked with an X to denote that it is to be cut. Use a pair of fine, sharp and pointed scissors to cut away the fabric. You may find it easier to work from the wrong side but you must make sure that the stitches are not cut.

Bars can be worked to bridge cut areas together. When you are running stitching around the design, as you reach the position for the bar, carry the thread across to the position opposite and take a small stitch. Take the thread back and take a small stitch. Bring the thread back to the opposite side. Work button hole stitches over the laid threads without catching the fabric underneath. When the bar is finished, continue with running stitch around the design.

Cut work with bars is traditionally called Richelieu work and is beautiful when worked on garments such as baby clothes, blouses and lingerie.

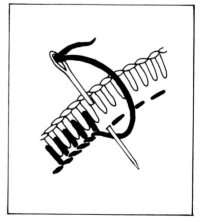

Double buttonhole stitch

Richelieu work uses bars to cut arrows. Buttonhole stitches cover laid threads.

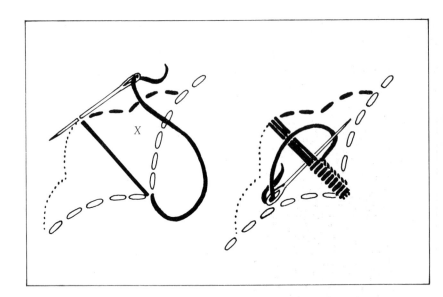

Picot edging can be added to the buttonhole bars

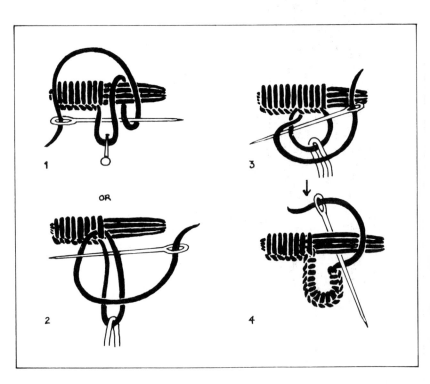

CUTWORK COLLAR

Detachable collars have been out of vogue in recent years but have definitely been making a comeback as more and more people remember or discover how useful they can be. On top of a blouse, they add a new look to an old garment and can make all the difference to a plain dress. They can even be tied on top of round-neck fine sweaters.

This isn't a project in the same way as most of the others in this book — but some suggestions for you to consider as you decide what type of collar you would like. The basic instructions are as follows.

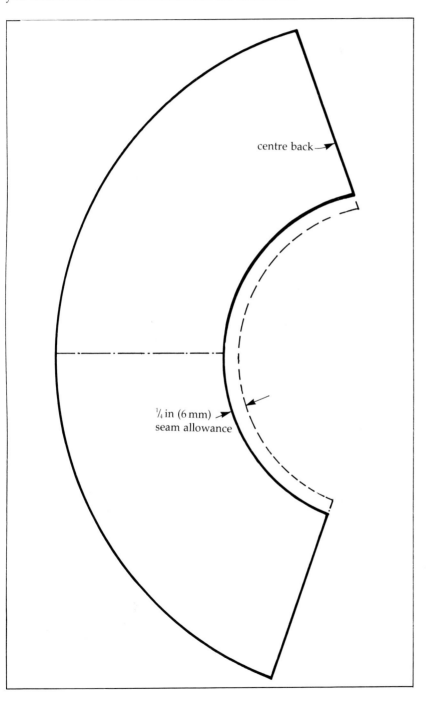

centre back

¼ in (6 mm)
seam allowance

Diagram 1

MATERIALS

1 yd (1 m) light weight fabric (fine cotton or linen is ideal).
White sewing cotton.
Tracing paper.

TO MAKE

1.   Using the tracing paper, draw and cut out the pattern given (diagram 1), remembering that the pattern should be reversed at the centre back to complete the collar. The easiest way to do this is to place the centre back line on the fold of paper. Try round your neck to check the size — alter if necessary to get a collar that sits comfortably about the neck and meets at the centre front. Cut two from fabric.

2.   With right sides together, pin, tack and sew the neck edge, using a $\frac{1}{4}$ in (6 mm) seam allowance. Clip into curve from seam allowance side and turn right side out.

3.   Press. Tack both layers together to hold securely as you work. And that's it — of course you have to add the embroidery now and decide about fastening. The easiest way is to add a small button and work a buttonhole loop, but you can add ties. You could also bind the raw edge of the neck with binding cut from the left-over fabric, extending the binding to form the ties. In this case, it isn't necessary to sew the neck edge together first.
   The depth of the collar is easily altered. For a 'cavelier' type collar, extend the width by another 3 in (7.5 cm) but work in exactly the same way.

IDEAS FOR FINISHING THE COLLAR

The easiest way (and the best way if you are a beginner) is simple scalloping along the edge. You can use a coin to get even scallops, but fit them round the paper pattern first to make sure that they all fit on. When you have transferred the scallop onto the collar, work around with running stitches and follow the general technique described earlier in this chapter. See also diagram 2 and 3.
   For more complicated effects, use a design that requires more careful cutting and the chance to use some other embroidery stitches to enhance the design. You may be able to get commercial transfers and patterns to fit the collar too.
   For a really simple effect, just round the collar point with a coin or small glass to draw an arc and buttonhole stitch all round. Add other embroidery if you want.

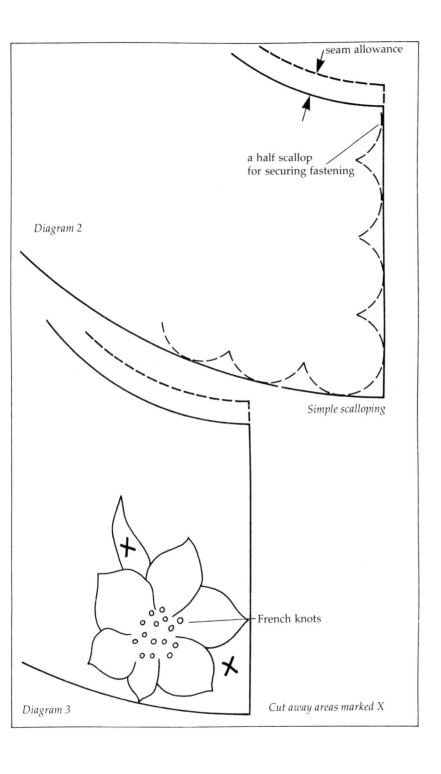

seam allowance

a half scallop
for securing fastening

Diagram 2

Simple scalloping

French knots

Diagram 3

Cut away areas marked X

CHAPTER TEN

OPEN WORK

The group of embroidery techniques called open work, include some very old and traditional methods that can be found in the earliest days of decorating and sewing fabric.

Called open work because areas of the background fabric are pulled or cut away, this type of embroidery has something in common with counted thread work as the effects are based on meticulous counting, and cut work, described in Chapter 9, is also known as open work.

The three main types of open work are pulled thread, drawn thread and Hardanger; the last two have fabric cut away or pulled out, whilst in pulled thread work, the stitches pull the fabric threads together.

PULLED THREAD

As each stitch pulls the fabric threads apart, open lacy patterns are formed without removing any fabric. These patterns are either used in rows to form borders or used to fill areas of a design. Worked areas can also form traditional motifs that form a centrepiece to the project.

Pulled thread work is used predominantly on household or decorative linens, but the technique can be used effectively for gift items and on garments as inset panels.

Even weave fabrics are best for pulled thread work as the threads need to be counted. A loose weave will give the best results — too firm a weave will not pull open properly. Traditionally, pulled thread work is done on white or natural linen or cotton, but the wide range of modern embroidery fabrics means that colours can be chosen to suit all needs. If you are using this technique on household items, remember that the finished piece will have to be laundered regularly, so chose an appropriate fabric. Large areas of open pattern may also be unsuitable as they are likely to catch and pull.

Most threads are suitable for pulled work as long as they are selected to match the weight of the fabric — a good rule of thumb is to use an embroidery thread that matches the weight of a single thread of the fabric. Pull one from the cut edge of fabric to compare.

Selecting a needle, follow the opposite to the usual rule. Instead of choosing a needle that passes easily through and is as small as possible, you will need a tapestry needle as large as possible that will still slip between the fabric threads — this will help exaggerate the pulled openings.

Use an embroidery hoop, but don't tighten the hoop or fabric so that the fabric is very taut. You will need some 'slack' to pull the stitches.

See the stitch directory for this chapter for pulled stitches — remember that the stitches are pulled evenly to group the threads together and will not look like the diagrams in the directory which can only show the stitch formation. This technique breaks another of the general embroidery rules — stitches are meant to be pulled tight and it would be a good idea to practice this first to get the right effect.

As you start to work, you should mark the centre of the piece with tacking or blue marker pen. Count out from the centre to place motifs and work in rows, turning the work if necessary to work a row in the other direction.

DRAWN THREAD

This type of open work embroidery has some of the weft and warp threads drawn out or removed from the fabric. The remaining threads are then sewn into groups with a variety of different stitches to create open, woven effects.

It is only really possible to work drawn thread work in borders or strips; the technique doesn't lend itself to figurative work although folk-type motifs can be worked by combining small strips. Because of this, drawn thread work is usually used on household linens and for decorative effects on tablemats, tablecloths and similar items.

Generally, only weft **or** warp threads are drawn out of the fabric but this means that corners where borders meet are left without any threads, giving a large square hole. These corners need to be reinforced, first with buttonhole stitches at the outer corners and then filled in with a decorative stitch to give stability.

Fabric for drawn thread work should be firm but with an identifiable weave. Threads need to be drawn out easily so a very firm or tight weave is not suitable. Even weave fabrics are suitable and will make thread counting much easier. As pulled thread work, drawn thread is most often used for table linen and similar items, so choose a fabric that launders well. Laundering can be difficult if the item has large areas where the threads have been removed — it can weaken the fabric. In these cases, where projects are planned using large drawn areas, it is important that enough decorative stitching is done to reinforce the fabric.

Thread choice and colour depends on the effect required — a fine thread the same colour as the fabric will give lace-like results whilst a thicker, brighter thread will give a less conventional, bolder result.

Use a tapestry needle to suit the thread — the needle isn't used to go through the fabric except to secure and finish thread.

The two basic groups of stitches used for pulled thread work are hemstitching and needleweaving. Threads are pulled from the fabric in the same way for both methods — the difference is in the way the remaining threads are sewn.

To draw out threads, decide how many threads deep you wish the sewn area to be. Centre this on your fabric or locate the area if it is to be a border. Tack along both edges of the area you have chosen with two horizontal threads. Mark the centre of the design or border with tacking. Use a pair of sharp, pointed embroidery scissors to cut the horizontal threads along the centre tacking. Using a tapestry needle, draw out the cut threads, leaving the vertical threads free and uncut. At the edge of the border or design, weave the cut end back into the wrong side of the fabric, following the weave of the fabric for at least an inch (2.5 cm). Trim threads.

The vertical threads are now free to be embroidered using the stitches in the directory for this chapter. The edges of the drawn area are usually

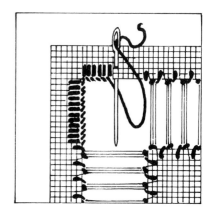

Corners are reinforced with buttonhole stitch.

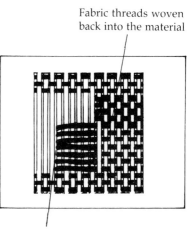

Fabric threads woven back into the material

loose, cut ends

hemstitched to stop the edge pulling and fraying. This can also include turning a hem on the item at the same time.

HARDANGER

This work is named after a region in Norway, although work of a similar type was done in Persia many centuries ago. It is recognised by the characteristic blocks of satin stitch that outline the motifs used.

The surrounding blocks of stitches hold the shape for weft and warp threads to be removed — unlike drawn thread work, both weft and warp threads are drawn out leaving a network of threads which are covered with stitches to make bars. The areas left between the bars can be filled with looped filling stitches that complete the design.

Like other forms of open work, Hardanger stitchery is usually seen on linen but can be worked to great effect as inserts in clothing and for smaller gift and decorative items.

Almost all even weave fabrics are suitable for this work. As the stitches are worked over an even number of threads, the finer the fabric weave, the smaller the worked motif will be. There is a specialist fabric available, called simply Hardanger, which consists of pairs of weft and warp threads and this is designed specifically for this work. Traditionally, Hardanger work was done with white thread on white fabric but the full range of embroidery fabric colours are used nowadays and Hardanger fabric can be found in a range of colours.

It is usual for two embroidery thread thicknesses to be used; a thicker thread for the outer 'kloster' blocks and a thinner for the work in the centre of the motif. Pearl cotton is often used, as is stranded cotton — both work very well. You can also experiment with different threads and fabric for less traditional effects.

Use a tapestry needle for sewing. You should also use a hoop or frame to keep work even.

The basic kloster blocks are composed of five satin stitches sewn over four threads of fabric (when Hardanger fabric is used, each double thread counts as one). The blocks are worked across in rows or on steps. They must be placed directly opposite each other around the motif or chosen design as they anchor the cut ends of the weft and warp threads that are removed from the centre. Once the blocks around the design are worked, cut the four threads at the base of each kloster block (ensuring that you cut the same four threads at the base of the opposing block). Remove the threads with tweezers. The remaining threads can be decorated using the stitches in the directory.

Designing open work   As the examples of open work given in this chapter all use counted thread technique, it is easy to design your own projects using graph paper. Use the grid of the graph to represent the woven fabric thread and plan the design and stitch placement. This is very valuable, since once the threads have been cut or pulled it is impossible to repair an error. Copy the design onto the embroidery fabric by tacking stitches.

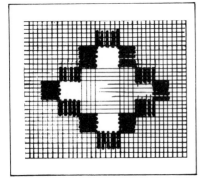

Traditional Hardanger shape.

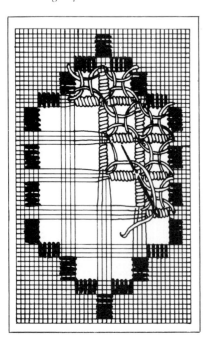

The remaining threads between the Kloster blocks are grouped and decorated.

STITCH DIRECTORY

PULLED THREAD

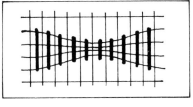

Satin stitch

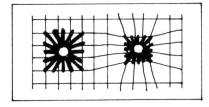

Eyelet

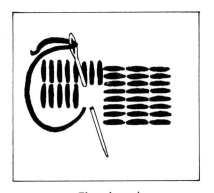

Chessboard

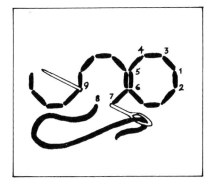

Ringed backstitch

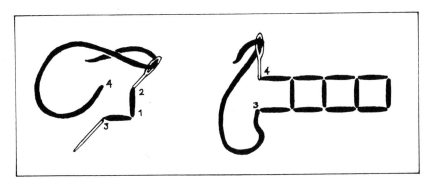

Four-sided stitch

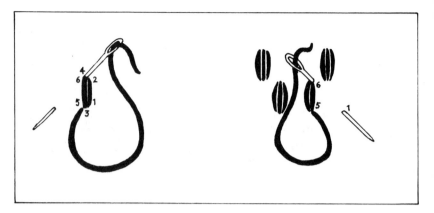

Coil filling stitch

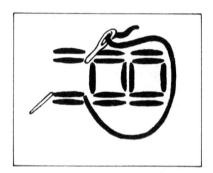

Framed cross stitch

Drawn Thread

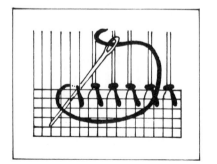

Basic Hemstitching

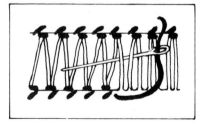

Hemstitch worked with different
thread groupings

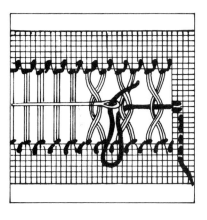
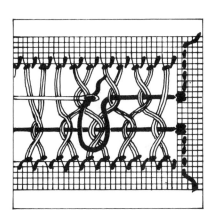
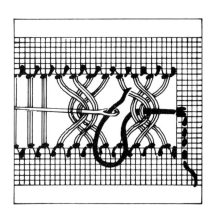

Twisted borders

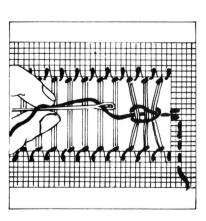
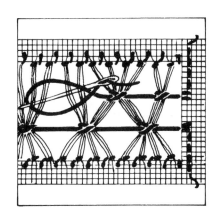

Single and double knotted borders

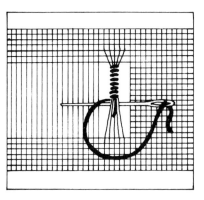
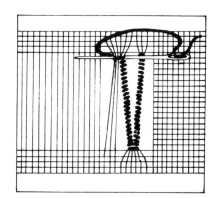
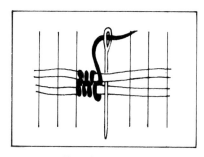

Overcast stitch   Overcast variation   Darning stitch

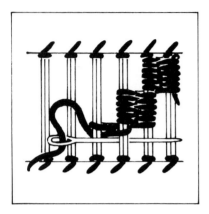
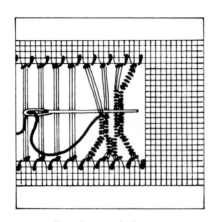
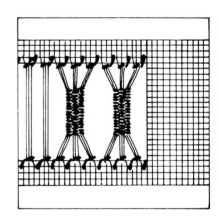

Darning variations

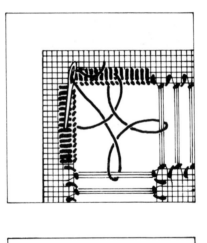
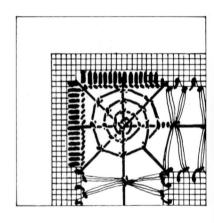

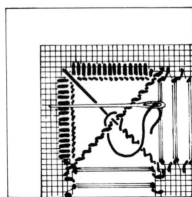
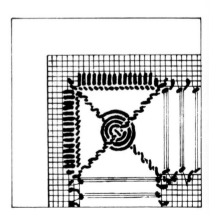

Filling open corners

HARDANGER

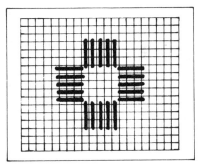

Kloster blocks

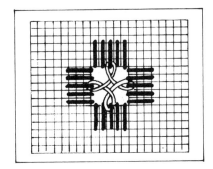

Straight loops

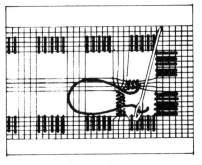

Woven bars

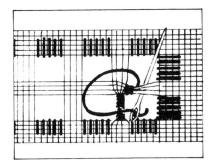

Overcast bars

CHAPTER ELEVEN

COUNTED THREAD

Almost all embroidery, apart from freestyle, uses counting of some type — usually the number of warp or weft threads that a stitch is worked over. So almost all embroidery, including cross stitch, open work (both separately covered in earlier chapters) and canvas embroidery (which is worked over a given number of canvas meshes) could be included in this chapter.

As these subjects have already been covered, we shall 'round up' the types of counted work not yet covered into this chapter with some general hints on working counted thread embroidery.

The common factor in all types of counted thread work is the basic fabric used. Even weave fabric is the best as this will guarantee that a motif will work to a consistent size and will also make counting for stitch location easier. Having restricted the choice to even weave, the restriction almost disappears again with the vast range of fabrics available. Again, traditional effects use a white or natural fabric with thread colours to suit, but the modern range of embroidery fabrics include a wide selection of colours and thread counts to the inch (2.5 cm) enabling you to co-ordinate any project as you choose.

Linen or cotton have been the most popular fabrics for this type of work, but there are weaves of fibres like wool and flannel that are also suitable, especially if you are working on a garment. Man-made mixes are also suitable, and should be considered if you need to launder the finished item regularly.

If you are not sure whether a fabric is suitable, accurately measure a square inch (or 2.5 cm) and carefully count the threads along and down. Measure again further along — if the thread count is consistent then you should be able to use it. If you have any doubts, work a sample piece to see if you are getting the results you require.

Recommending threads for counted work is almost impossible given the variety of background fabrics that can be used — general advice is to balance the fabric with the thread and use threads that pass easily through the fabric without pulling and distorting it. Use a tapestry needle as this will pass between the threads of the fabric. Remember to choose a suitable thread if the finished item is to be washed — metallic threads and more experimental threads may not launder well.

Many of the commercial designs for counted thread work show the native and folk background of many of the stitches — which were originally used on national costume and household items. If you want to design your own motifs or patterns, use graph paper and transfer to the fabric with tacking stitches or blue marker pen. If the lines will be completely covered with stitching, you can use something more permanent for marking the design area.

BLACKWORK

Blackwork is a striking form of counted thread embroidery traditionally worked in black thread on white or a light coloured fabric. It is often seen in

Elizabethan portraits, when it was a popular form of fabric decoration and used to add to the rich opulance of dress of the wealthy.

It is widely regarded as originating in Spain and its popularity during Tudor times was encouraged by growing links with Spain. Historically true or not, blackwork has an 'old' look which can be very cleverly balanced with simple forms and shapes for a project full of variety and life.

Blackwork consists of small, straight stitches arranged in patterns over counted threads, giving regular motifs in different densities. It can be worked to form pictures or decorative objects and on household linen, clothing and accessories. It isn't essential that large areas are worked, as you only need a small piece of blackwork to get the effect and it can be included as a band or panel or set, for example, into the lid of a fabric box.

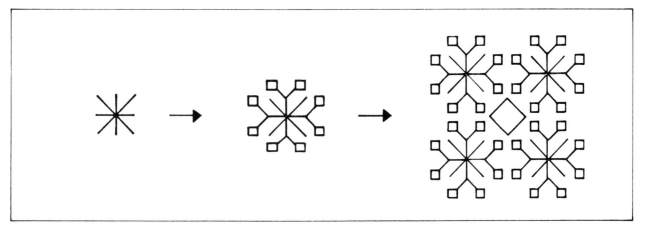

Blackwork stitches and patterns are built up in stages — this pattern starts with an Algerian eye stitch.

Even weave fabric is ideal for blackwork as it is easy to work and will give a consistent stitch size. You can use other plain weave fabrics, but it will be less easy to guage stitch size and the patterns formed will not be so even. The thread count of the fabric will affect the size of the patterns and stitches formed, so choose a fabric that will suit the required finished effect or item.

As a rough rule, an embroidery thread to match a single fabric thread is suitable, but because blackwork uses density to match tones that would be there if different colours were used, you will need to vary thread thickness to get very light or dense effects. Threads as fine as machine embroidery thread may be used, whilst tapestry wool at the other end of the scale can be used for very dark areas. It is not advisable to use this large range of threads on one piece — three thicknesses will probably be suitable; on a simple scale, two, four and six strands of stranded cotton will get good results.

Nowadays, embroiderers don't restrict themselves entirely to black. Other, dark colours can be used on light fabrics, whilst light colours can be used on a dark background fabric. Touches of another colour, like red with black or metallic gold or silver can add great interest too.

The different densities and effects of light and shade are achieved by

Blackwork designs need to have simple shapes and clear outlines — this fruit layout is ideal.

using different stitches that can be built up to achieve darker and lighter areas. The same stitch can have a totally different effect if worked in a light thread than if worked with crewel or Persian wool. Stitches are usually worked over two, three or four threads and can be added to with other stitches laid on to build the effect. Running stitch, back stitch and double running stitch are used to outline shapes.

Designs for blackwork need to be simple in outline as complex shapes do not lend themselves to rendering in this type of embroidery. Plants, fruits, buildings in simple form are all good subjects, especially if you choose suitable stitches — some stitches will lend themselves to brickwork or leaves and will give the feeling of the area being worked.

Use a tapestry needle. A hoop isn't essential, but you may find it helpful!

to have the work stretched out. The temptation with this technique is to forget the two-motion stitch where the needle is inserted in one movement and passed back through the fabric in another but it should be used to achieve evenness and a regular tension.

Blackwork stitches include running, back and counted thread stitches found in the directories for earlier chapters. See the directory for this chapter for blackwork stitch patterns.

PATTERN DARNING

This is another method of counted thread embroidery and can be worked in very simple patterns or complex weaving. It can resemble weaving when completed on some fabrics as it uses horizontal or vertical running stitches that follow the warp or weft of the fabric used.

These results are obtained on even weave fabric where the stitches are worked over and under different amounts of threads so accurate counting is essential.

Complex patterns can be built up by varying the number of threads to form jacquard patterns; the smaller the gaps the denser the pattern. Thread choice will also influence this; single threads like pearl cotton or tapestry wool will lay on the surface giving a raised pattern, whilst finer threads like strands of stranded cotton or crewel wool will lie flat with the weave of the fabric, letting the fabric show through.

Less common forms of pattern darning are Huckaback and net darning. Huckaback is a type of towelling fabric that has thread 'floats' in the weave that run vertically down the fabric on the surface. These floats can be sewn through without penetrating the fabric, leaving a darned pattern lying on the surface.

Although common some years ago. Huckaback is a technique that has gone out of fashion but is now beginning to gain popularity again. Designs are usually geometric, although simplified forms of people and animals can be worked. Borders for items like guest towels are easily worked whilst motif placement for more complex patterns need working out in some detail. Most darning designs are worked in rows of stitches that start at the bottom and are built upwards, but it's helpful to start the first row from the centre out to make sure that the design fits and is properly located in the centre of the fabric. This is particularly important when the design consists of repeated motifs, where you will want to fit in as many complete motifs as possible.

Although used for linen and some decorative projects, Huckaback can also be used as inserts in garments and can be very effective on clothes for children.

Stitches used are straight running stitches or loops that go up and down into rows of floats above and below. See stitch directory for more details.

Huckaback fabric isn't easy to get hold of (try contacting the specialist suppliers at the back of the book if you are having trouble locating this fabric). Aida fabric, intended for counted cross stitch, makes an excellent substitute. The blocks of four threads that are woven into a basketweave

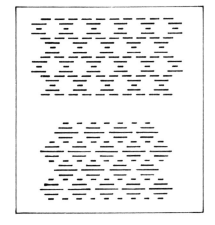

Woven patterns made from pattern darning.

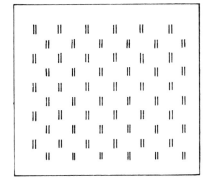

Pairs of thread 'floats' lie on the surface of Huckaback fabric, forming a regular pattern.

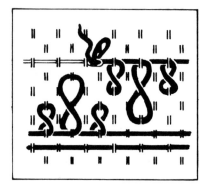

Patterns are woven through the floats without piercing the fabric.

effect leave two stitches on the surface that can be picked up in the same way as the floats on Huckaback. Even weave linen can be used but will need careful planning to be used successfully.

Net darning uses the grid formed on net fabric (used for curtains and some dressmaking) as a basis for darning a thread in and out. This involves counting threads along or up and down and can achieve very good results, transforming a very plain fabric into something special. The results can be used as net curtains, or, if done on a small scale, backed with a contrasting colour fabric for cushions etc.

(The type of net darning done in Europe weaves the embroidery thread in and out of the grid to fill in solid blocks of coarse net. Although effective, this really doesn't fall into the category of 'counted thread').

STITCH DIRECTORY

BLACKWORK

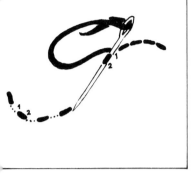

Double running or Holbien stitch

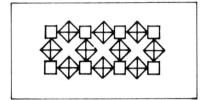

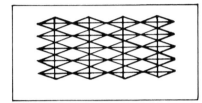

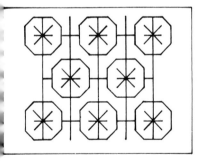

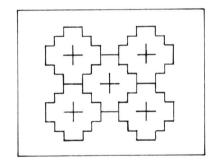

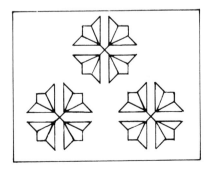

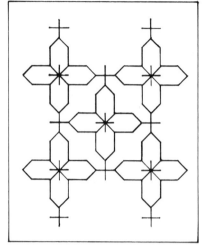

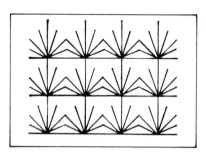

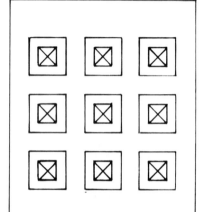

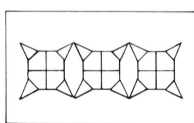

Pattern darning

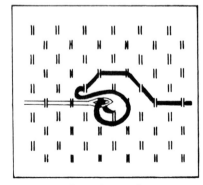

Straight stitch

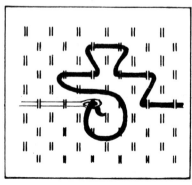

Offset

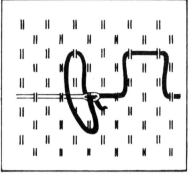

Open loops

Closed loops

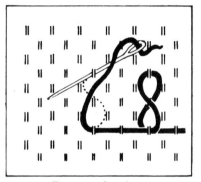

Figures of eight

Geometric runner.

GEOMETRIC STYLE

This table runner is worked simply using a few counted stitches on even weave fabric. The geometric design could also be used successfully on table mats and napkins, whilst you can experiment with stranded wool for a bolder effect.

MATERIALS

Anchor stranded Cotton:
Black 0403   4 skeins
Grey 0400   3 skeins
Amber Gold 0309   2 skeins
Grey 0398   2 skeins
Use 6 strands for 0398 and outer border only in 0403.
Use three for rest of embroidery.
½ yd (40 cm) white even weave embroidery fabric, 21 threads to the inch (2.5 cm), 60 in (150 cm) wide.
No. 20 tapestry needle.

TO MAKE

1.   Cut a piece of fabric 39 in × 16 in and mark the centre both ways with a line of tacking stitches or a blue marker pen. Finish the edges to prevent fraying.

2.   Work the embroidery following the chart and using the colour and stitch key. The chart gives a section of the design (A), with a corner turning (B) — the blank arrows indicate the centre and line up with the centre line of tacking stitches.

Diagram 1
The diagram shows the arrangement of the stitches on the threads of the fabric represented by the background lines.

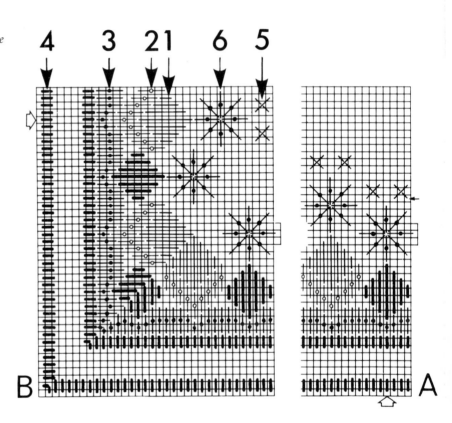

1 — 0309 ⎫
2 — 0398 ⎬ SATIN STITCH
3 — 0400 ⎪
4 — 0403 ⎭
5 — 0309 — CROSS STITCH
6 — 0400 — STRAIGHT STITCH

STRANDED COTTON

3.   The design is commenced with a long side facing at the small black arrow, 75 threads down and three threads to the right of the crossed tacking stitches. A is worked 19 times more to the left of the centre, then the corner section B is worked. Continue the design sequence to length wise tacking stitches. Work the remaining three quarters in the same way.

4.   Press embroidery on the wrong side.

5.   Trim fabric to within 2¼ in (6 cm) of embroidery and turn an inch (2.5 cm) hem, mitring corners as you stitch, (diagram 2).

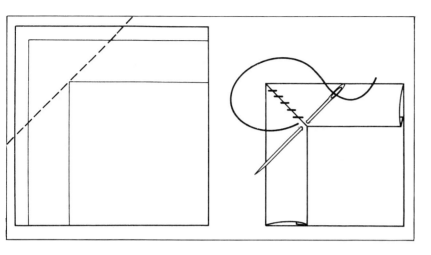

Diagram 2
Cut away surplus fabric before finishing
corners with a mitre.

WINDOW TREATMENT

This net curtain, worked in very simple running stitch, is probably the easiest project in this book but makes a stunningly different window treatment. The instructions are for a curtain 45 in (114 cm) wide but it is very easy to add or omit motifs to suit other widths. A different gauge net will also produce different results. Want to co-ordinate with a colour scheme? Select a thread colour to suit perhaps in size 5 or 3 pearl cotton.

MATERIALS

Anchor Stranded cotton:
White 01 (14 skeins).
24 in (60 cm) white net with approx. 13 threads to the inch (2.5 cm) and 46½ in (118 cm) wide.
Required length of white, fine Terylene net curtain, 46½ in (118 cm) wide.
No. 20 tapestry needle.
Drima polyester thread.
Tapestry frame with 27 in (68 cm) tapes (optional).

TO MAKE

1. Mark the centre of the narrow width of the net with a line of tacking stitches. The net can be mounted on a frame but be careful not to pull the net too tightly or the embroidery will be distorted when it is taken off the frame.

2. Follow the diagrams and work the embroidery using enough thread in the needle to ensure that a complete motif can be embroidered at a time. To end and start threads, weave under several worked stitches, following the darning pattern.

It is easy to extend this pattern for a larger window — add motifs until you have the required width. Make sure you have enough thread in the needle to complete a motif.

Diagram 2

This layout diagram shows the complete lower section of the curtain, showing the position of the embroidered insets.

3.   The diagrams give a repetitive section and a section of the borders for each design, A and B. Blank arrows indicate the centre of the design and coincide with the tacking stitches.

The diagrams also show the arangement of the stitches on the threads of the net represented by the background lines. The layout diagram shows the completed lower section of the curtain with shaded areas and letters representing the embroidered inserts.

Design A. With one long side of the net facing, commence the design at blank arrow, 15 in (38.5 cm) from the lower edge and, omitting the borders, work the section as given. Repeat twice more to the right and three times to the left, working the far right side to correspond with the far left side with one more figure motif to the right. To complete, work the borders as given, starting at the right hand narrow end.

Design B. With one long side of net facing, commence the design at the blank arrow 4¾ in (12 cm) from the lower edge and, omitting the borders, work the section as given. Repeat twice more to the left and right. Work the far left side to correspond with the far right hand side with three more motifs to the left. To complete, work the borders given, beginning at the right hand narrow end.

4.   Press the embroidery very lightly if required when finished.

5.   To make up, cut out strips as shown plus ⅝ in (1.5 cm) seam allowance on each piece and ¾ in (1.5 cm) for side and lower hems. When inserting embroidered strips, tack and sew right sides together. Trim seams and neaten edges.

At top edge, cut curtain to required length plus seam allowance and finish as desired.

Window treatment.

CHAPTER TWELVE

MACHINE EMBROIDERY

With the increasing sophistication of home sewing machines, all sorts of techniques and results are now possible — including programmed embroidery stitches of different sizes and effects.

Although these automatic machines can produce attractive stitches, it isn't necessary to have one of these sewing machines to embroider by machine. Even the most basic version can be used for free motion embroidery. (For a description of free motion embroidery see later in this chapter).

Machine embroidery is very versatile and can be used on almost any type of fabric. Very thin fabrics can be backed with paper to add strength as you sew — the paper is pulled away when sewing is complete. Again, match the fabric to the stitch and the thread — and the style of the finished project — to get the right balance.

Many of the sewing thread ranges include machine embroidery thread on spools. This is a slightly thicker thread than the usual dressmaking thread and is available in a wide range of colours. Top stitching thread is also available; this is a bold thread used for decorative top stitching on garments. You can also hand or machine wind embroidery threads like pearl cotton onto spools or bobbins, but this requires patience and some machines may be temperamental and not accept this. Use your sewing machine handbook for further advice.

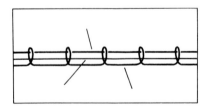

Once you can control your machine properly and turn corners neatly, this type of border is easy to work by machine.

If you tighten the stitch tension, the bobbin thread will be pulled through to the wrong side, forming a thread 'bead' on the right side of the fabric.

STRAIGHT STITCHING

The most basic machine can be used to create embroidered effects, using bold thread and experimenting with stitch and bobbin tension and using different stitch lengths for the best results.

To get good results, the main skill is to be able to turn corners properly and control curves.

To turn a corner, stop at the end of the line where the corner needs to be turned — as exactly as possible. Stop with the needle in the fabric. Lift the presser foot and turn the fabric, pivoting on the needle. Lower the presser foot and continue stitching.

Controlling curved sewing is often a question of speed — it's much easier to follow a curve at a slow speed than when the needle is racing away. Take the curve slowly and control the fabric as evenly as possible. The line will probably be less jerky if you can sew the curve in one go without stopping.

Use a heavy thread for borders and use a suitable stitch length to emphasize the embroidery. Mark the design on the fabric as carefully as possible to keep the border even and follow the drawn line as closely as possible.

By adjusting stitch and bobbin tension you can also create some unusual effects; tighten the stitch tension slightly and the bobbin thread will be pulled through onto the right side of the fabric, making a small thread bead. Reduce or disengage the bobbin tension and hand wind a thick thread like coton pearl onto the bobbin. Working from the wrong side stitch slowly; thread loops will be formed on the right side. This technique of winding a bobbin with a heavy thread can also be used to produce a couched effect. Loosen the bobbin tension and tighten the upper tension. Stitch from the wrong side to give a couched appearance on the right side.

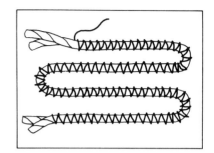

Couching with zigzag.

ZIGZAG STITCHING

The facility to do zigzag stitching is available on most modern machines. Your machine handbook will show you how to use the zigzag facility for satin stitching and buttonholes as well as the basic zigzag stitch.

To turn a corner accurately stitch to end of the line at the corner to be turned, stopping with the needle still in the fabric at the outer edge. Lift the presser foot, pivot and turn the fabric on the needle, lower the presser foot and continue stitching. The new line of stitching will cover the end of the first line.

For special effects try: filling an area with cross hatching lines of stitching by sewing horizontally, vertically and then diagonally; couching over thick thread or cord with a wide set zigzag stitch (laying the thread as you stitch); tighten the top tension to get a wishbone effect as the bobbin thread is slightly pulled through to the right side of the fabric.

The zigzag stitch can usually be set to form a tight satin stitch — this can be used for machine sewing decorative borders and can also be used for machine appliqué (where a different coloured motif is applied to a background fabric with satin stitch at the outer edge of the motif).

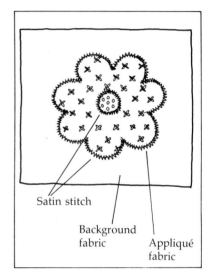

Satin stitch

Background fabric

Appliqué fabric

Machine appliqué

AUTOMATIC MACHINES

These very sophisticated machines are programmed, either by the user selecting particular controls on the machine or pre-setting by the manufacturer, to stitch complicated embroidery stitches. Your manual will show the best way of producing these. Enhance the effect of these stitches by sewing over contrasting bands of ribbon or couching down a cord or thick thread. Experiment with different threads for the surface and bobbin — remember that if you use a special thread in the bobbin which you want to show, you will have to sew on the wrong side of the fabric.

FREE MOTION EMBROIDERY

This technique of using a sewing machine offers a fluidity of movement and design that is otherwise unavailable with the straight lines of machine sewing.

The fabric can be moved freely as the presser foot is not used and the feed underneath the fabric is either covered or lowered. The fabric is placed in an embroidery hoop (which is used upside down) and can be moved around in any direction — all the control is in moving the hoop. The stitch effect is created with different thread tension and types. It is important that you read the instruction booklet for your machine before starting this type of embroidery. The information given here is general and should be used in conjunction with the handbook.

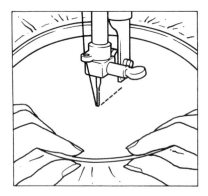

Note that the hoop is used differently to hand embroidery and that the presser foot of the machine has been removed. The important technique is to keep the hoop moving.

Remove the presser foot from the machine (and the shank that holds it in place if this can be removed). Cover up or lower the feed plate on the bed of the machine. Set the stitch width to the lowest possible and loosen the stitch tension slightly.

Put the fabric in the embroidery hoop — placing the fabric and any backing right side up over the larger (top) hoop. Put the smaller ring inside the large ring keeping the fabric flat and under even tension. Lower the presser bar to stitch, holding the upper thread taut and slowly engage the bobbin loop through the fabric. Pull out the bobbin thread so that both threads lie on the top of the fabric. Take a few stitches holding both threads and trim the ends closely when the threads are secured. Sew the design, manoeuvring the hoop to follow any design lines and going at an even speed (not too fast!). Keep the fabric moving unless you want a group of built up stitches.

Remember that the stitch length is controlled by machine speed and the speed at which the hoop is moved. Although it is tempting to use a large hoop, 8 in (20 cm) is an optimum size and the hoop should be moved onto unfinished areas when one area is finished. Also make sure that the needle takes the thread thickness comfortably — if the thread or needle is unsuitable it will lead to thread breakage and difficulty in keeping a flowing movement.

It is also possible to use satin stitch in free motion embroidery by setting the satin stitch and moving the frame very slowly so that the stitches are formed closely together. Stitch width can be varied by using the stitch width lever.

If you want to fill a shape with satin stitch, move the hoop from one side of the shape to the other and back again. Keep the hoop moving, rotating it to move from one part of the design to the other. To shade, work several rows of satin stitch with irregular edges so that the next block of colour will blend without leaving a hard line.

Cut work on a large scale can also be done, using the satin stitch of a zigzag machine. It can also be done in a free motion way but this takes some skill and is not an easy technique for the beginner. Follow the outline of the design with a straight stitch and then cover with satin stitch (following the principles of the hand technique but using a machine). Trim the open areas away with sharp scissors.

Small designs will be difficult to work and as the satin stitch is heavy, most fabric will benefit from backing with iron-on interfacing.

CHAPTER THIRTEEN

OTHER TECHNIQUES

It would be a Herculean task to cover all forms of embroidery in detail in this book — most of the individual types are of such scope that they can be found covered exhaustively in books or publications devoted to them alone. The best that this book can do is whet your appetite for embroidery in all its manifestations and give you some starting points. Although this guide has covered most of the principle forms of embroidery, there are some styles or types that because of space (or that they are variations of other techniques) have had to be left to this chapter of 'miscellaneous' ideas and techniques.

PLASTIC CANVAS

A fairly new introduction from America, plastic canvas replaces the conventional fabric canvas used for canvas embroidery and cross stitch. Made, as the name suggests, from plastic, it is available as rigid sheets of mesh that are used for embroidery with wools or several thicknesses of finer threads to form very stable pieces of embroidery that are very quick to work.

It can sometimes be purchased from a roll or as precut shapes about 2½ in (6.5 cm) in diameter) of squares, hexagons, diamonds, circles and ovals. These precut shapes are very good for Christmas decorations and similar items. Meshes of 3, 5, 7 and 10 meshes to the inch (2.5 cm) are made, but 7 and 10 are the most popular and therefore the most widely available. The 'canvas' is easily cut with scissors (taking care to remove any spikes of plastic).

Any canvas embroidery stitch can be used, using a no. 20 tapestry needle for most projects. Charts for plastic canvas work are available (look for Dover and Leisure Art books, American publications that are available in this country — some specialist suppliers in this country can also supply 'home grown' products and ideas) and ordinary canvas projects can be adapted.

Plastic canvas works up very quickly and is very suitable for either young children or adults who find that, perhaps through illness, they can no longer handle fine work.

Because it is worked on such a rigid background, finished panels of plastic canvas are ideal for making into items like tote bags, tissue box covers, note book covers, photo frames and baskets. The panels are easily lined, too.

RIBBON EMBROIDERY

Once a Victorian pastime and worked on sentimental floral pieces, ribbon embroidery is currently making a return to favour, aided by the wide variety of colours and sizes of ribbons available.

Ribbon can be used for embroidery in two ways; either sewn through the fabric in the same way that embroidery thread would be or laid on the surface and stitched over — in effect, couched, with thread to keep it in place.

Ribbons for sewing should be narrow and used in conjunction with

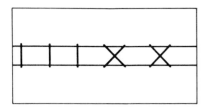

To couch ribbon, lay it on the embroidery fabric and pin in position if the ribbon is to be laid in straight lines. Otherwise, hold the ribbon in place as you work, following curves or design shape. Stitch over at regular intervals using straight stitch, cross stitch or lazy daisy. You can also work the length of the ribbon, covering it in an open stitch like herringbone. Make sure that the stitches are frequent or the ribbon will snag and pull.

either a loose weave fabric so the ribbon can pass easily through or passed through the fabric via a small hole made with a large needle or stiletto. Ribbons made by Offray that are either $\frac{1}{16}$ in or $\frac{1}{8}$ in (1.5 mm or 3 mm) wide are excellent for sewing with as they are very narrow and of good quality, with a wide range of colours. Wider ribbons can be used with some practice and can be couched on to great effect. Narrow ribbon is also excellent as a thread for sewing on plastic canvas.

Ribbon embroidery should be worked and regarded as normal embroidery and worked on a hoop and finished to suit the eventual purpose of the piece.

CANDLEWICKING

This technique is also popular in America and is seen to some extent in this country.

It owes its background and appearance to the pioneer days of America when material for embroidery and decoration were few and far between. Coarse linen was available, as was the fibre used to make wicks for candles; these were combined to form candlewicking, an embroidery of knots in natural colours on an unbleached linen fabric. Although the name seems familiar to us from candlewick bedspreads, the true results are quite different.

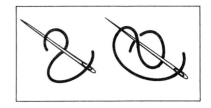

Colonial Knot is a bolder stitch than a French Knot and is used extensively for candlewicking.

Nowadays, candlewicking is usually done on unbleached calico, using a cream coloured thread. Some specialist embroidery suppliers will be able to supply American candlewick thread, but other suitable substitutes are stranded cotton, pearl cotton and cream Danish flower thread. The traditional result is best achieved with a matte thread.

The outlines or shapes are worked with a variation of the French Knot and are now combined with other freestyle stitches. Designs are usually based on motif or embellishing the natural shape of a cushion or finished item rather than figurative work, but candlewicking can be effectively combined with shapes stencilled with acrylic paints for a real folk-art look.

BEAD EMBROIDERY

Much of the beaded embroidery we see, perhaps in museums or old family pieces, have a truly dated feel, as the Victorian times were the heyday of this form of embroidery. The way that beads can be added or used for embroidery can vary. The most popular way is for beads to replace either isolated parts or complete areas of stitchery on canvas — where a stitch would otherwise be located, a bead of the correct size and colour is used. In past times they would be used extensively to build up a complex, shaded picture.

This technique is still used today, although perhaps less lavishly than our Victorian ancestors. Some modern cross stitch charts now include bead highlights to add variety and texture, whilst experimental pieces of a more abstract nature may use a wide range of beads of differing size and material.

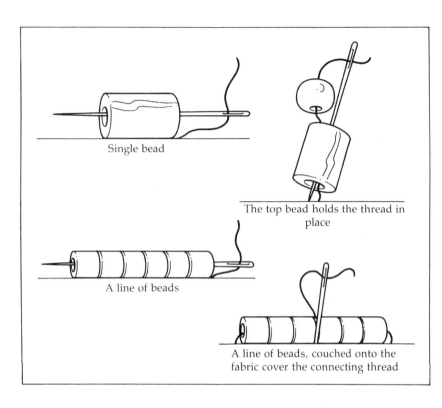

Single bead

The top bead holds the thread in place

A line of beads

A line of beads, couched onto the fabric cover the connecting thread

Bead weaving is a technique that originated with the American Indians and is done on a simple loom. This produces a flat piece of beading which can be added to bags, belts and jewellery. The beads are woven on several at a time running under and over the warp and weft threads.

When using beads as part of embroidery, it is a good idea to strengthen the thread with beeswax — the beads may have a cutting edge which would eventually work through the holding thread.

SHADOW WORK

The delicate and fine embroidery is worked using fine threads on fabrics that are transparent or semi-transparent like silk, organdie and very fine lawn. This method uses herringbone stitch to fill in areas of a design or border from the reverse side of the fabric, leaving the shadow of the stitches to show through the fabric and a line of small back stitches showing on the right side. This is very effective using white thread on white fabric but pastel colours also work well, with a very pale coloured image showing from below with the true thread colour providing the outline on the right side.

Wide areas of motifs or borders are not advisable — if the herringbone stitches are too long, as they are liable to catch. Complicated designs are also difficult to work; simple, closed shapes are best. Some surface stitchery can also be used to enhance the design.

Shadow work can look beautiful worked on lingerie, bridal wear and on delicate items like handkerchief sachets.

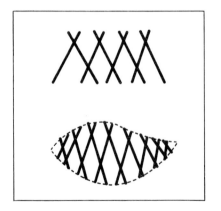

Herringbone stitch worked inside a shape from the wrong side. Small backstitches outline the shape from the right side.

STOCKISTS

Branches of the John Lewis Partnership usually stock a good selection of embroidery materials in their haberdashery departments.

If you have trouble locating the specialist fabrics referred to in the text, Zweigart fabric is distributed by Dunlicraft Ltd., Wigstone Road, Leicester. They will be able to put you in touch with a local supplier.

The following shops and suppliers offer a mail order service. Look in your local Yellow Pages for shops in your area. Embroidery, published by The Embroiderer's Guild, is a magazine with extensive advertising from specialist suppliers.

Needle Needs,
20 Beauchamp Place,
Knightsbridge,
London SW3
Tel: 01–589 2361

Richmond Art and Craft,
181 City Road,
Cardiff CP2 3JB
Tel: 0222 490119

Voirrey Embroidery,
Shop: Brimstage Hall,
Brimstage,
Wirral.

Mail Order: 18 Hilary Drive,
Upton,
Wirral,
Merseyside L49 6LD
Tel: 051 677 7393

Mace and Nairn,
89 Crane Street,
Salisbury,
Wiltshire SP1 2PY
Tel: Salisbury 336903

Spinning Jenny,
Bradley,
Keighley,
West Yorkshire BD20 9DD
Tel: 0535 32469

Leven Crafts,
23 Challoner Street,
Guisborough,
Cleveland TS14 6QD
Tel: 0287 39177

Christine Riley,
53 Barclay Street,
Stonehaven,
Kincardineshire AB3 2AR
Scotland.
Tel: 0569 63238

The Workbox,
8 New Arcade,
High Street,
Uxbridge,
Middlesex.
Tel 0895 55985
(Please telephone before ordering)

Magpie's Embroidery Centre,
Broad Street Place,
Broad Street,
Bath,
Avon.
Tel: Bath 62176

The following businesses specialise in books on embroidery and needlecrafts or locating them to order.

The Bridge Bookshop,
7 Bridge Street,
Bath,
Avon.
Tel: 0225 66152

Four Shire Books,
17 High Street,
Moreton-in-Marsh,
Glos. GL56 0AF

Sacketts,
34 Dorset Street,
Blandford Forum,
Dorset.
Tel: 0258 53837

John Ives Antiquarian Books,
5 Normanhurst Drive,
Twickenham,
Middlesex TW1 1NA

CLASSES

On a national basis, hobby/interest classes are organised by local education authorities at day or evening classes. More details can be obtained from the Adult Education Department of your local education department.

The Royal School of Needlework offers courses on a professional and vocational basis and organises some classes on behalf of the Inner London Education Authority. Send a stamped self addressed envelope to Classes, RSN, 5 King Street, London WC2 8HN.

The City and Guilds association organises courses through colleges and further education centres that lead to recognised qualifications in embroidery. For further details contact:

City and Guilds,
46 Brittannia Street,
London WC1
Tel: 01–278 2468

One day courses and short stay residential courses are also organised at many adult education colleges throughout the country. The following colleges usually include courses in their prospectus that are suitable for the home embroiderer. Contact the colleges concerned for their programme.

Missenden Abbey Adult Education College,
Missenden Abbey,
Great Missenden,
Bucks HP16 0BD

Nelson and Colne College,
Gawthorpe Hall,
Padiham,
Burnley,
Lancs.

Styal Workshop,
Quarry Bank Mill,
Styal,
Cheshire SK9 4LA

Theobalds Park College,
Bulls Cross Ride,
Waltham Cross,
Herts.

The Earnley Concourse,
Earnley,
Nr. Chichester,
Sussex.

The Old Rectory Residential Adult Education College,
Fittleworth,
Pulborough,
Sussex.

West Dean College,
West Dean,
Nr. Chichester,
Sussex.

Degree courses leading to a Bachelor of Arts in Embroidery or specialising in embroidery are available at some art colleges and centres of higher education; look for further details in the reference section of your local or main library.

ORGANISATIONS

The two major organisations for embroiderers are:

The Royal School of Needlework (for address see Classes).
The RSN is a delight for all embroiderers. It has a shop on the premises that stocks a large selection of materials and accessories (plus another shop in Libertys', Regent Street, London, and runs a comprehensive selection of courses. They will also undertake private commissions. The workroom teaches full time students. It is possible to become a Friend of the School and support their work.

The Embroiderer's Guild,
Apt. 41A,
Hampton Court Palace,
Surrey.
Tel: 01–943 1229

The Guild is an educational charity, open to all interested in the craft of embroidery. There are local affiliated branches in Great Britain which have their own programmes and events. The Guild also organises the Young Embroiderers' Society for those under 18.
The Embroiderers' Guild organises courses throughout the year and publish a quarterly magazine that is a goldmine of suppliers, news and events. The magazine can be obtained through subscription or ordered through local newsagents and branches of WH Smith if not kept on display.

AMERICAN SUPPLIERS

All these companies will supply by direct mail order or provide details of local stockists.

C. J. Bates and Sons,
P.O. Box E, Route 9A,
Chester CT 06412
(Susan Bates, Anchor threads)

Coats and Clarke Inc.
P.O. Box 1010,
Toccoa, GA 30577
(Coats thread)

Craft Gallery,
P.O. Box 541,
New City, NY 10956
(DMC thread)

Charles Craft Inc.
P.O. Box 1049,
Laurinburg, NC 28352
(Embroidery fabric and general supplies)

Regency Mills,
Phillipsburg, NJ 08865
(General materials and equipment)

Boycan's Craft and Art Supplies,
P.O. Box 897,
Sharon, PA 16146
(General supplies and equipment)

Hansi's Haus,
35 Fairfield Place,
West Caldwell, NJ 07006
(Fabric)

BIBLIOGRAPHY

50 Counted Thread Stitches.
50 Freestyle Stitches.
100 Embroidery Stitches.
Published by J. and P. Coats Ltd.

Embroidery by Mary Gostelow.
Published by Marshall Cavendish Editions.

Cross Stitch Samplers by Jane Kendon.
Published by Batsford.

Embroidery Stitches by Barbara Snook.
Published by Batsford.

Embroidery by Diana Springall.
Published by the BBC.

The Complete Guide to Needlework.
Published by Reader's Digest.

Bargello — Florentine Canvas Work by Elsa S. Williams.
Published by Van Nostrand Reinhold.

INDEX

How to make the most of your talents…

…get Popular crafts every month